HTML Publishing

WITH Internet Assistant

YOUR GUIDE TO USING MICROSOFT'S HTML ADD-ON

HTML Publishing
with Internet Assistant

YOUR GUIDE TO USING MICROSOFT'S HTML ADD-ON

Gayle Kidder & Stuart Harris

VENTANA
PRESS

HTML Publishing With Internet Assistant: Your Guide to Using Microsoft's HTML Add-on
Copyright © 1995 by Gayle Kidder & Stuart Harris

Library of Congress Cataloging-in-Publication Data

Harris, Stuart (Stuart H.)
    HTML publishing with Internet Assistant : your guide to using Microsoft's HTML add-on / Stuart Harris & Gayle Kidder. --1st ed.
        p. cm.
    Includes bibliographical references and index.
    ISBN 1-56604-273-9
        1. Hypertext systems. 2. HTML (Document markup language) 3. Microsoft Internet assitant 4. World Wide Web (Information retrieval system) I. Kidder, Gayle. II. Title.
QA76.76.H94H373 1995
005.75--dc20

                                                95-18699
                                                CIP

Book design: Marcia Webb
Cover design: Tom Draper Design
Vice President, Ventana Press: Walter R. Bruce III
Art Director: Marcia Webb
Design staff: Brad King, Charles Overbeck, Dawne Sherman
Editorial Manager: Pam Richardson
Editorial staff: Angela Anderson, Jonathan Cato, Beth Snowberger
Project Editor: Lynn Jaluvka
Print Department: Wendy Bernhardt, Dan Koeller
Production Manager: John Cotterman
Production staff: Patrick Berry
Index service: Richard Evans, Infodex
Proofreader: Angela Anderson
Technical review: Eric Leach

First Edition 9 8 7 6 5 4 3 2 1
Printed in the United States of America

Ventana Communications Group, Inc.
P.O. Box 13964
Research Triangle Park, NC 27709-3964
919/544-9404
FAX 919/544-9472

Trademarks

Trademarked names appear throughout this book and on the accompanying disk. Rather than list the names and entities that own the trademarks or insert a trademark symbol with each mention of the trademarked name, the publisher states that it is using the names only for editorial purposes and to the benefit of the trademark owner with no intention of infringing upon that trademark.

About the Authors

Gayle Kidder and Stuart Harris coauthored the highly successful Ventana title, *Netscape Quick Tour* (Mac & Windows versions).

Gayle is a journalist and editor with 20 years' experience in books, magazines and newspapers. She has published more than 500 articles in magazines and newspapers on topics as diverse as science, theater, art, travel, fiction and literature, and computers. She currently maintains an online column of cultural events for the city of San Diego at **http://www.thegroup.net/kidder/otsd.htm**.

Stuart is the author of *The irc Survival Guide* (Addison-Wesley, 1995), chapters in *Internet Secrets* (IDG 1995) and *Cyberlife!* (SAMS, 1994) and numerous articles about the Internet in national magazines. He works as an Internet consultant and is leader of his local computer society's Internet special-interest group. He has also been involved in technical editing and TV documentary production. He enjoys communicating complex ideas to a mass audience.

Apart from coauthoring *Netscape Quick Tour*, the authors' joint projects have included TV documentary production, journalism, software product management and, recently, a type of live theater on the Internet. Gayle and Stuart work in the classic "electronic cottage" near the beach in San Diego and are on the Net every day of their lives.

Acknowledgments

First up to the acknowledgment dais, please, our sysadmin Mark Burgess of the Data Transfer Group. Mark proves on an almost daily basis that sysadmins can be lovable as well as knowing a hell of a lot.

Kevin Horst is Microsoft's own guru on the Internet Assistant for Word (as it's officially known) and has plenty to do in the course of a day without being pestered by e-mail from authors. He nevertheless helped us a great deal in understanding his baby.

Some of the "corporate graphics" used for the pages of our mythical World Wide Widget Corporation were in fact designed by the Intersé Corporation for one of its clients. We thank Terry Myerson for permission to give them a fictional life as well as a practical one. JB of Ultramedia Design here in San Diego also provided some widget graphics and guided us toward some useful graphical references.

We consider Web sites in general to be in the public domain, so we don't feel obliged to give special mention to everyone whose home page we used as an example for this book. We thank them all generically, but with special mention for those who gave extra information and encouragement:

- Neil Thompson of the Natural History Museum, London
- Joop Schilleman of the Technical University of Eindhoven, The Netherlands
- John Leavitt of the Center for Machine Translation, Carnegie Mellon University
- Chris Pearce of Europa, Honorary Curator of the Enhanced for Netscape Hall of Shame

To all those adventurous Web pioneers who help to make the Web an interesting place to be by freely sharing resources, designs and encouragement, a big all-embracing thank you. May your spirit prevail as the Web continues to grow.

Contents

Introduction

Since you've bought this book (or are standing in the aisles of your favorite bookstore contemplating whether to buy it), it's a safe bet that you've had reason to become intrigued with that growing phenomenon, the World Wide Web. As the fastest-growing segment of the Internet today, the Web has managed to turn what started as an elite military-scientific-technical network into a worldwide community as diverse and various as all human interests. From financial information to Grateful Dead fanhood to genealogy research—the Web's got it all. And what it hasn't got, somebody's probably plotting this very moment. (Who knows? Maybe that guy reading over your shoulder right now in the bookstore aisle.)

You may have already decided to become part of the gold rush of the '90s and stake a claim in your own little corner of the Web. Maybe you've got a little project already in mind—a collection of useful information you'd like to share, an advertising opportunity for your business, a class project or an art project that reaches beyond the lonely confines of your studio or gallery. Whatever it is, you want to design your own Web pages and get them on the Web for the whole plugged-in world to see.

In this book, we'll show you how to do just that. You'll learn to create smart-looking Web pages the painless way, with nothing but your friendly word processor and a little help from your friends on the Web.

Internet Assistant for Word—we call it Word IA in this book—is a free add-on program for users of Microsoft Word, version 6.0a or higher. It allows users to create documents in Word or convert existing documents in Word for publishing on the World Wide Web. It also allows you to cruise the Web straight from Word, without ever loading another program, by means of a special Web browsing component that's never more than a click away.

Chances are you're already familiar with Word, although you needn't be terribly sophisticated at document preparation. We assume you have at least an elementary understanding of the Internet and some exposure to the World Wide Web, probably through another Web browser like Mosaic or Netscape. But you needn't have any understanding whatsoever of HyperText Markup Language (HTML), the code language of the Web. Word IA takes care of all that for you, and by methodically going through the process of page creation with you, we'll explain what you need to know.

So what are you waiting for? Let's go.

Hardware & Software Requirements

If you're already a Word user and have had a little experience on the Internet, you probably already have what you need to use Word IA. The basic requirements are as follows:

- A 386 or 486 computer with at least 6mb RAM (8mb is better).
- Word for Windows 6.0a or higher (a free upgrade patch is available for Word 6.0).
- MS-DOS 3.0 or higher.
- Windows or Windows for Workgroups version 3.1 or later. The software will also work with Microsoft Windows for Pen Computing.
- 2mb hard disk space.
- Microsoft Mouse or compatible pointing device.
- 14,400-baud modem or better.
- An existing Internet connection.

A word about those last two items: it's perfectly possible to use Word IA to create and read hypertext (HTML) documents over a local area network (LAN) without an Internet connection. You can also create documents without an online connection. But in order to use Internet Assistant over the World Wide Web, you'll need either a direct Internet connection through your institution or business or a SLIP or PPP connection, either of which you can get for a reasonable cost from a private access provider. If you're setting up for the first time, you'll need a TCP/IP stack (such as Trumpet Winsock), which your access provider should be able to help you get and configure.

Super–duper Quick Start

If you're already a fully qualified Web user with an up-and-running Web connection, you'll probably be anxious to get started creating your Web pages. So for those of you with ants in your pants, here's how to get a head start:

Go straight to "Installing Word IA" in Chapter 1. Follow the instructions for installing the program from the disk at the back of the book. When installation is complete, choose the Launch Word option. The readme.doc that comes up on your screen will give you basic information on the program.

Click on the little eyeglasses icon that's been added to the extreme left of your Formatting toolbar. This displays the Web Browse screen. You can call up any HTML file you have on hand—something you saved from another Web browser, say. Make the connection to your online service and saunter off for a look at some of your favorite Web sites. If you need help navigating, dip into Chapter 5 for an overview. If it's a little slower than the Web browser you're used to, remember that Word IA's real power is in the way it lets you create Web documents with all the ease and comfort of Word commands. If you have another Web browser, you'll probably find creating your documents in Word and checking them with your regular Web browser to be a comfortable match.

When you're ready to settle down and create a page, click on the pencil icon (which replaces the eyeglasses icon in Web Browse View). Then jump back to Chapter 2, where class is in session. If you find the beginner level too remedial, go straight on to Chapter 3, where we talk in more depth about all the Web editing commands that Word IA puts at your fingertips, or go to Chapter 4, our "intermediate HTML" course, where we begin to have some more advanced fun designing Web pages.

What's Inside

We've tried to organize this book to make the material easily accessible, no matter what your level of computer experience or knowledge of the World Wide Web and HTML. If you're new to HTML and the Web, you'll want to start with the background material in Chapter 1 and the "beginner's course" in creating your first home page in Chapter 2. If you're a little more knowledgeable and have had some experience creating Web pages, you'll be able to skim this material to pick up what you need, then start getting your hands dirty in Chapters 3 and 4. In the later chapters, we go on to some advanced topics that even fairly experienced HTML authors should find helpful in enlivening their Web pages. Chapter by chapter, here's what you'll find:

* Chapter 1, "The Wonderful Web," gives a brief overview of the Web and Web resources for the benefit of readers whose experience of the Web is minimal. We explain what the World Wide Web is and why it has become the fastest-growing segment of the Internet in the last few years. Then we march on to explain what you need to get connected and how to install Word IA. To familiarize you with the program, we take a quick peek at the new menu options Word IA adds to your Word screen, as well as the two different screen views that Word IA gives you.

* In Chapter 2, "Your First Home Page," you'll learn how to create an elementary Web document by following our simple example for the World Wide Widget Corporation, a

small company that thinks big and wants to get online and make itself available to the world. This example will grow with us as we advance our Web page authoring skills, and we'll enhance it with examples from other areas of interest. We'll save the text for later refinements as we learn more about creating Web pages.

- Chapter 3, "The Edit View," takes a closer look at all the options on your menus and toolbars for HTML editing. This chapter will serve as a useful guide and ongoing reference that you can come back to any time.

- Chapter 4, "Using Images & Links Creatively," shows how to insert images into documents. We'll illustrate graphically how to use different kinds of links and give you some ideas for arranging your family of documents in order to create a complete Web site.

- Chapter 5, "The Web Browse View," takes a look at the Web browsing features of Word IA. You'll learn how to navigate the Web and how to mark your favorite places for easy return. Along the way, you'll learn how to find and copy examples from other Web pages that you might like to use on your own page.

- Chapter 6, "Converting Word Documents to HTML," shows how to take existing Word documents—company press releases, brochures, newsletters, teaching materials, what have you—and turn them into Web documents. We'll discuss what works online and what doesn't, and we'll explain how to doctor your documents for a better Web presentation. You'll learn how your hyperlinks should look and how to fix problems you might have with them.

- Chapter 7, "Advanced HTML Options," tells how to create forms for user feedback. We'll take a look at sensitive maps, which can add a sophisticated graphical element to your pages. Then we'll talk about how to add exciting new dimensions to your Web pages with audio and video.

- Chapter 8, "Tips & Tricks," contains lots of interesting inside info about things the pros do to smarten up their

Web pages. It includes some of the fancier design features you can use with Netscape and tells how to make interlaced and transparent GIFs (image files in Graphic Interchange Format). Finally, we'll help you get ready to post pages on the Web.

In the back, you'll find an appendix to help you access the *Internet Assistant Online Companion*, which is full of useful resources like companion software and hot links to Web resources, including icon libraries and HTML editing guides. In the other appendices, you'll find handy references to HTML tags, special characters and color coding.

Next Stop—the Web

As the Chinese philosopher Lao-tzu said, "A journey of a thousand miles must begin with a single step." Actually, as we all know, it begins with packing. Fortunately, we've taken care of that for you. We've packed the disk you need to get started right in the back of this book. And we've also packed a trail mix of useful material in our handy online companion, which you can dig into whenever you need a little help.

There are just a few other things, though, that you might find useful to take along:

- curiosity—the bigger the dose, the better
- a spirit of adventure
- a sense of humor—always a useful item to have when you venture out into new territory

We've got a long way to go. So take the disk out of the back of the book, and let's get started!

Gayle Kidder
Stuart Harris
San Diego, California

1

The Wonderful Web

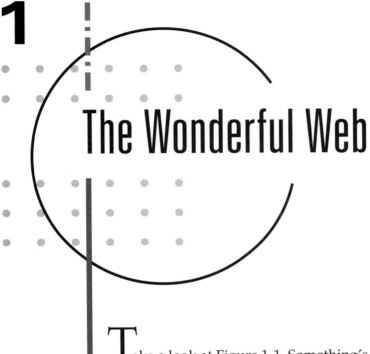

Take a look at Figure 1-1. Something's growing faster than mold on a three-day-old club sandwich!

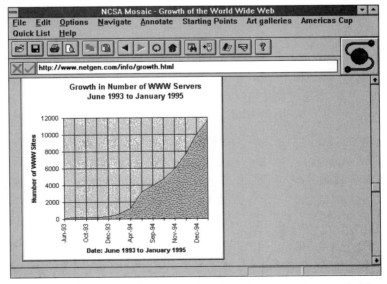

Figure 1-1: *Exponential growth of the World Wide Web, recorded by Matthew Gray of net.Genesis (Cambridge, MA).*

Well, that something is the number of computers that interconnect to form the World Wide Web—a phenomenon that didn't exist at all until 1989, and wasn't heard of outside a tight clique of techies until the Mosaic Web browser was released in 1993. To say that the Web then became popular quickly is a bit like saying that *Jurassic Park* didn't do too badly at the box office—it doesn't quite do justice to the phenomenon.

Webs & Nets

The jargon of the Internet is confusing, to be sure. There are FTP and irc, WAIS and Gophers, Veronicas, Archies and Jugheads, TELNET, USENET and BITNET. Mostly these are just protocols for handling data exchange and for presenting the vast amount of information in the form of a manageable number of choices to us, the users of the Net.

The fact that there are so many protocols is an indication of how the Net grew up, with nobody in charge and a lot of opinionated people imposing their ideas on different segments of it. (Of course, the Internet is quite different now—NOT!)

The appeal of the World Wide Web is twofold: First, it promises to bring most of the important protocols within one package, putting its own style on all of them, much as Microsoft Windows imposes a common style on applications as different as spreadsheets and games of solitaire. Second, it brings with it yet another protocol, the HyperText Transfer Protocol (HTTP), which allows easy linking of text, pictures, movies and sound in such a way that users can pick their own paths through the body of available data.

And what a body! Matthew Gray, who is responsible for the Web page shown in Figure 1-1, is no longer certain that his software, The Wanderer, can count the number of Web sites accurately. As for the number of hypertext *pages* out there, plus their ancillary hypermedia files—well, they've been beyond counting for quite some time.

So although the Web is really part of the Internet, it looks so different that you'd hardly know it. Once Mosaic became available for personal computers, and Internet connections became more commonly available, the word spread like wildfire: Hey! You can visit the Library of Congress or the palace of Diocletian; you can dissect a frog, read a newspaper or contribute to an ongoing sculpture—all without leaving your desk, and at practically no cost! First scientists, then librarians, students, journalists, businesses and just plain folk, more or less in that order, got connected and started absorbing information in a whole new way.

Mosaic & Other Animals

The first graphical Web browser, Mosaic, was the creation of a government laboratory—the National Center for Supercomputing Applications at the University of Illinois, Urbana-Champaign. Undoubtedly part of the attraction was that it was a US government product, free and guaranteed to stay that way. Figure 1-1, showing the growth of the Web, is actually a screen from the Windows version of Mosaic 2.0.

The NCSA FTP site was beseiged for weeks as people downloaded Mosaic to their computers. Mosaic was so popular that it soon inspired others. Air Mosaic, Spyglass Mosaic, WinWeb, Cello and Netcom's Netcruiser are all spin-offs, as is the latest Web marvel, Netscape. (Out of habit we very nearly put a hyperlink to our own Ventana book, *Netscape Quick Tour*, in there—this conventional printed-page stuff is so limited!)

NCSA itself, however, has not rested on its laurels. Having replaced the young brains who went off to earn good money at Netscape Communications Corporation from the inexhaustible supply of students, NCSA Mosaic keeps the new versions coming, and still has the advantage of being guaranteed free.

Word IA: Your Passport to the Web

The Web has democratized information exchange as never before. Not only can anybody with the right software and connection get information from the Web, but anybody with just a little more access can create his or her own page; give it an address that Web computers all over the world can recognize; maintain, improve and connect it to other people's pages; and participate in a way that makes reading a newspaper suddenly seem like a passive way of becoming informed.

Once you get up and running with Word Internet Assistant (Word IA), look around the Web. Along with pages at the Smithsonian and the great museums of Paris and London, you'll come across thousands of pages that have titles like "Dave's Home Page" or "Claire's CD Collection" (see Figure 1-2). To be sure, not all of these very personal pages are worth reading. The point is that their status is equal to that of the Smithsonian—the Web is a game anybody can join, including you and your business, school, church, class, club or kids. All it takes is a little creativity.

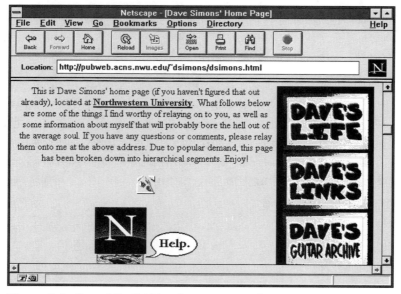

Figure 1-2: *One of the funkiest home pages we've come across.*

Up to now, though, there's been one slight snag. A Web page has to be written in a certain way to function correctly on the Web as one strand in the vast skein of hypertext that crisscrosses the globe. Just as printers need to understand type fonts, and TV directors need to know about camera angles and lenses, so a hypertext author needs to know how to mark up a page with instructions for its display, such as "this is a level 2 heading," "put a picture of a daffodil here," "start a numbered list of things here" or "link this word to a document on a computer in Tokyo." The set of instructions that defines the display of a Web document is called HyperText Markup Language—HTML for short—and these instructions have been agreed upon by an international group of computer developers and programmers. Most Web page authors need to be familiar with 20 or 30 HTML elements, which are known as *tags*.

If that general idea sounds familiar, it's because text markup is exactly what advanced word processors like Word for Windows do to create the look of a brochure or a form. If you examine a Word document byte by byte, you won't see the illustrations, font changes or indents. Instead, you'll see embedded references to these things that don't appear to make any sense at all. You cannot interpret them at that level because they are written in a code you don't need to know.

Word IA brings this same principle to the creation of HTML documents. If an HTML author wants to make the word *life* a link to a computer in London, the raw text might look like this:

```
<A HREF="http://www.nhm.ac.uk:80/exhib/lifeg/
lifeg.html">life</A>
```

As a user of Word IA, you can create that code simply by using the Hyperlink option on the Insert pull-down menu. Of course, you still need to know the Web address of the Life Galleries at the Natural History Museum, but the Hyperlink option sure makes the process easier (see Figure 1-3).

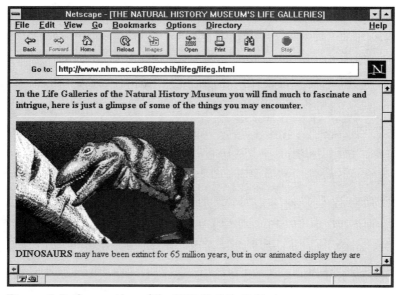

Figure 1-3: *One section of the NHM's Life Galleries page.*

Web Addresses & How to Read Them

That address for the London Natural History Museum is technically known as a *Uniform Resource Locator* (URL). It consists of five separate parts, as do most of the URLs you will come across.

http:// is the *protocol,* in this case HyperText Transfer Protocol. Other possibilities are ftp://, telnet://, gopher:// and mailto:.

www.nhm.ac.uk is the address of the host computer. "nhm" obviously means "Natural History Museum." Less obviously, "ac.uk" means an academic institution in the United Kingdom.

:80 is the port number on that computer. This is nearly always omitted, since 80 is the default for http data anyway. You may find occasional variants.

/exhib/lifeg/ is the directory path of the file you need.

lifeg.html is—finally!—the file itself. This is obviously not an IBM computer, since the file extension is .html rather than .htm. Actually, it's a Sun SparcStation, now running the Web server as a sideline, but soon to be dedicated to this famous museum's Web information services.

Looked at this way, the Internet Assistant appears to be just a customized version of Word that includes a fancy template and some new menu options. Actually, that's very close to the truth—but it's not the *whole* truth. To give you worldwide access to the famous Web, Word IA is all the above plus an interrelated Web browser rather like Mosaic or Netscape.

Getting Connected

To use the Web browsing feature of Word IA, or any other graphical Web browser for that matter, you will need a SLIP or PPP connection to the Net (for more on these, see the sidebar, "TCP/IP, SLIP & PPP"). If you have only a dial-up UNIX shell account, that word *shell* will take on another meaning as you shell out more money (but not much more) to your Internet service provider (ISP) for the upgrade. If you have no Internet access at all, you're going to be limited in what you can achieve with Word IA.

You really need an Internet connection. We mean it. Trouble is, there are so many possible options that we can't give sensible specific advice that would be helpful in your city and your situation. These days, every city in the United States has several ISPs to choose from, with more setting up shop all the time. A SLIP account typically costs about $25 per month.

Fortunately, a nice man named Peter Kaminski runs a free service called the "Info Deli." He keeps tabs on all public dial-up services and regularly updates a national listing that he calls PDIAL. To get it, send e-mail to **info-deli-server@netcom.com**, with the simple but effective message SEND PDIAL. What's that? You don't even have *e-mail?* Ah, the ultimate bootstrapping problem. You'll just have to find somebody who does, to help you take that first step.

TCP/IP, SLIP & PPP

Yes, Internet acronyms are confusing. Don't blame us. Here's a possibly helpful rule of thumb: Everything that ends with a *P* is a *protocol*, meaning an agreed way of exchanging information.

One of the most fundamental features of the Internet is packet switching, which simply means that all messages are broken down into packets and routed independently to their destinations. The most common protocol for managing packet-switched data (and you can readily imagine that some rules are desperately needed if messages are to be reassembled correctly) is known as *TCP/IP*, or Transmission Control Protocol/Internet Protocol.

TCP/IP does not come naturally to your PC or Mac, which is used to more mundane serial protocols like the XMODEM, YMODEM and ZMODEM protocols that are fine for talking to a bulletin board or a UNIX shell account. However, your desktop computer can be taught packet switching by adding a so-called TCP/IP stack and a program that allocates so-called sockets. Conventional modem connections are not up to handling data this way, which is why you need either a SLIP (Serial Line Internet Protocol) or PPP (Point-to-Point Protocol) connection to your Internet service provider. PPP, as the more modern protocol, is more efficient, and if your computer (the client site) is properly configured, your Internet applications won't even know which protocol is being used. Your best option depends much more on how the server is configured—which translates to "do whatever your sysadmin recommends."

Farewell, sweet UNIX!

Another Upgrade?

If you already have what you need for Microsoft Word, you probably won't need a hardware upgrade. Word IA is not one of those applications that comes along and, like Pac Man, gobbles up all in its path. Look again at the system requirements in the introduction to this book—these days, the requirement for a spare 2mb of hard disk space is considered almost trivial. We can remember achieving miracles with just a pair of 320k floppy disk drives, but that was in the days when software authors wrote economical code. Don't get us started!

One detail worth checking, though, is your version of Microsoft Word. On the Word menu bar, click on Help, then About Microsoft Word (for keyboard jockeys, Alt+H/A). The first line in the info box identifies your version. If it's 6.0a, 6.0b, 6.0c or later, you're in the clear. However, if it's just plain old 6.0, you need a little upgrade—and the good news is, it's free. What you need is called a *patch*, and Microsoft makes it available free for registered Word users. You can download the file free from Microsoft's FTP site at **ftp.microsoft.com/Softlib/MSLFILES/**. (For more on FTP, see the sidebar "FTP: You Mean It's Free?")

Or, if you prefer, you can order it for free on disk by calling Microsoft Sales Information Center at 1-800-426-9400.

The file is called word60a.exe. Put it in a temporary directory and run it in DOS by entering the command **word60a** at the c:> prompt. It unpacks to a readme file, a binary file and a setup batch file. Run setup using the Windows File/Run option from the Program Manager. Installation takes about one minute.

WARNING

*If you're running a workstation or network version of Word 6.0, or if you have any version other than the US version, do not use the word60a.exe patch file. If you have a Web browser, refer to Microsoft's Web page for current instructions (**http://www.microsoft.com/**) or call Microsoft tech support.*

Installing Word IA

Word IA is a breeze to install. During installation it adds the necessary menus and toolbars to your customary Word screen to allow you to begin writing HTML documents immediately. Before installing it, however, we recommend you close any Windows applications you have running. Then proceed as follows:

1. Remove the disk from the back of the book and insert it in your a: or b: disk drive.

2. To install Word IA from DOS, type **a:setup** (or **b:setup**) at the c:> prompt. The setup program will start Windows. To install from Windows, choose the File/Run option from the Program Manager and type **a:setup** (or **b:setup**).

3. You're presented with the license agreement and asked to Agree to its terms to continue.

4. Now you have the option of installing the program in the default directory, a subdirectory of the one in which Microsoft Word is installed (normally, the default would be c:\winword\internet). To install to a different directory, choose the Change Directory button and enter what suits you. When you're all ready, choose Continue.

5. The installation program asks if you want to install the Internet browsing components of Word IA. To get the full benefit of using Word IA, choose Yes. If space is limited and you intend to use only the editing functions or plan to write HTML documents for a local network installation only, you can choose No.

The hard choices are behind you. Settle back, and the actual installation begins and ends in little more than a minute. When it's done you can choose to launch Word immediately by clicking on that option when it's presented, or choose Exit Setup to return to the Windows Program Manager. If you launch Word immediately, the readme.doc (which gives information about the program) will be loaded for you.

Be sure to remove the disk from your disk drive and store it in a safe place. You may need it if you want to reinstall Word IA (should files get corrupted) or remove it from your system in the future.

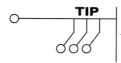

TIP

Use the same procedure to install Internet Assistant on a network. Be sure to install Word IA on the same server where Word for Windows is installed.

Reinstalling or Uninstalling Word IA

HTML work is not everyone's cup of tea, and—who knows?—you may find that it's not for you, or you don't have enough RAM after all. If you *do* decide to uninstall Word IA, insert your installation disk in your disk drive and follow the instructions for installation. The installation program will search for installed components on your hard drive and after finding them will give you the option to Reinstall or to Remove All.

Choose Reinstall if you need to restore corrupt or missing files. Choose Remove All to remove Word IA from your system and return Word to your previous setup. The setup software will ask if you are really sure about this, but will put on a brave face when you tell it to self-destruct.

Getting Updates

Word IA is very new, evolving software. Chances are that in a few months or a year you'll want to obtain updated versions. The current version of the software is available at Microsoft's FTP site for downloading free by FTP.

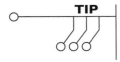

TIP *You can also order a copy of Internet Assistant on disk by calling the Microsoft Sales Information Center at 1-800-426-9400. The product will be mailed to registered Word users for a cost of $5.50 for shipping and handling.*

If you're new to the idea of FTP (and do not have a Web browser with FTP capabilities), we suggest you start with a simple FTP package, which you can get from your system administrator or access provider. We use a shareware program called WinFTP, but there are others.

Before you download Word IA, prepare your system by creating a temporary directory into which you can download the file. Now make your SLIP or PPP connection to the Internet, launch your FTP or Web browser software and go to this FTP site: **ftp.microsoft.com/deskapps/word/winword-public/ia**.

The notation we use in the line above, and throughout this book, is the generally accepted way of showing complete directions to an FTP site. The part before the first slash is the actual address of the FTP server, and the rest is the directory tree on that server, leading to the file you want. If you're using a Web browser with FTP capabilities (such as Netscape), simply precede the above address with **ftp://** in the URL box.

Download the following files into your temporary directory:

README.DOC	11 KB
WORDIA.EXE	1068 KB

Figure 1-4 shows the file transfer process using WinFTP, and Figure 1-5 shows the same thing using Netscape's FTP routine. The time needed for transfer is about the same in both applications, and is inversely proportional to your modem speed.

Once you have the file, unpack it by running the wordia.exe program. Then run setup from your temporary directory to install.

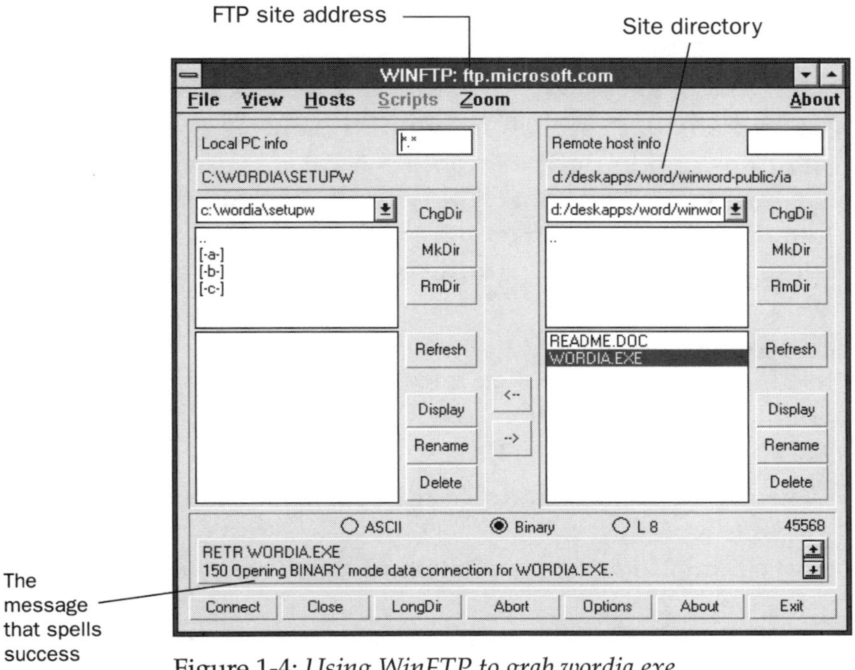

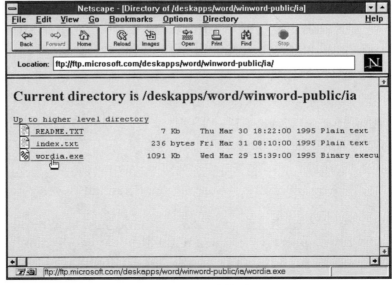

FTP site address

Site directory

The message that spells success

Figure 1-4: *Using WinFTP to grab wordia.exe.*

Figure 1-5: *The same process as it would look using Netscape.*

FTP: You Mean It's Free?
FTP (File Transfer Protocol) is one of the oldest ways of transferring information on the Internet. What it means is that you can access an archive on a remote computer and transfer a file lodged there to your own computer. No, not any file—this isn't hacking! FTP archives are purposely set up to be accessible to outside users. You access these archives by logging in as "anonymous" and using your e-mail address for the password (which is why it's often called *anonymous FTP*). This procedure is usually taken care of for you by FTP software packages. There are three ways of doing FTP:

- Through a UNIX system or shell account using UNIX commands as follows:
  ftp ftp.microsoft.com/deskapps/word/winword-public/ia
  or
  ncftp ftp.microsoft.com/deskapps/word/winword-public/ia

- With a Windows-based software package (such as WinFTP). Enter the address, pathway and file name in the appropriate places, according to the software instructions.

- With a Web browser with FTP capabilities, such as Netscape, use the URL address:
  ftp://ftp.microsoft.com/deskapps/word/winword-public/ia

Word IA's Two Faces

When you run Word IA, you're really running a combination of two powerful software applications that cleverly have been made to interact for your benefit.

One of them is Word for Windows itself, with the addition of two specially designed templates that help create HTML documents. The other is actually an adaptation of a product called InternetWorks, a very well-reputed Web browser created by a company called BookLink Technologies, Inc. InternetWorks was sold lock, stock and barrel to America Online, and BookLink became NaviSoft, Inc.—but not before Microsoft licensed enough of its code to create the Web browsing part of Word IA.

That little bit of background perhaps helps to explain a crucial fact about Word IA—that is, that it gives you two completely different views of your HTML documents. The components are so separate, actually, that you can choose not to include the Web browser in your installation, and you'll get just the editing tools.

- ❧ *The HTML Edit View*—The HTML Edit screen looks like a customized Word screen. On this screen you can edit documents, but you cannot browse the Web. You can insert hyperlinks, as your new menu promises, but you cannot follow them anywhere.

- ❧ *The Web Browse View*—The Web Browse screen has a rather different look, reminiscent of the InternetWorks screen, with big buttons bearing names that will be unfamiliar at first (for example, Add Favorite and URL). This screen is the converse of the Edit View—you can now link to the Web (assuming you have a SLIP or PPP Internet connection), but you can't do more than minor editing here.

Changes to Your Word Screen

Figure 1-6 shows the standard Word menu bar and toolbars before (top) and after (bottom) installation of Word IA. You have to look hard to spot the difference. One extra button has appeared—the one with the little pair of eyeglasses on it, at the extreme left end of the Formatting toolbar. That's the button you can now use to switch between HTML Edit View and Web Browse View. To make room for it, the Borders button has been pushed off the right-hand end, but you can still invoke the special bordering toolbar by selecting View/Toolbars from the menu (or Alt+V/T from the keyboard) and checking Borders in the toolbar list.

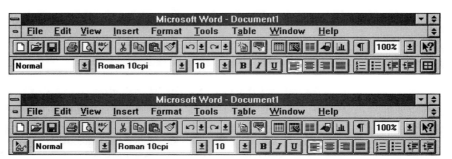

Figure 1-6: *Spot the difference: how your toolbars change.*

However, there are more changes than you can see by gazing at the screen. Some of the pull-down menus have already changed, and more changes will appear, both in the menus and the toolbar, when you load an HTML document. We'll go into the details in the next chapter. For now, note the new item tacked onto the Insert menu, which enables you to insert a hyperlink, and the new Browse Web item on the File menu.

A Whole New Look

If you choose Browse Web right now, Word will not only switch to Web Browse View (exactly as the new toolbar button does) but will also autoload a document called default.doc (see Figure 1-7). The file default.doc is not truly an HTML file (they are invariably pure ASCII text, and almost always have extensions .htm or .html). But it behaves like a so-called home page in many ways. When you come across an underlined word or phrase in color (blue is the default), you can click on it to go to a different document, which in turn has its own clickable phrases. This is the world of true hypertext, and the colored phrases are the hyperlinks. You should already be familiar with this concept from using your Word Help menu. This ability to skip from one document to another searching out detail is the very essence of the World Wide Web.

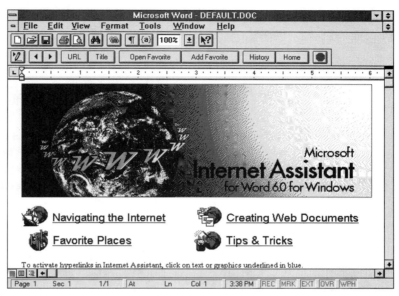

Figure 1-7: *The Web Browse screen, with default.doc loaded.*

Almost all of the hyperlinks you can access from default.doc are local—that is, they are contained in other files in your own computer. They're part of the kit you just installed. But some are external. If you've made your SLIP or PPP Internet connection before loading default.doc, click on Favorite Places and you'll find a link to cool places to get you started. You'll soon find yourself saying to your imaginary companion, "Toto, I don't think we're in Kansas any more." Figure 1-8 depicts the telltale sign that you are leaving Kansas far behind and setting off into the wild blue yonder of the Internet. You can return any time you like by pressing the back arrow button, which will take you back to the previous screen. You can also close Word down at any point and then close your Internet connection.

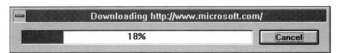

Figure 1-8: *The page load info box: a sure sign that you are loading a remote file.*

Moving On

We hope that in this chapter we've managed to bring Web-newbies quickly up to speed and give them an appreciation for the many fascinating dimensions of the World Wide Web, which Word IA makes it easy for you to contribute to.

We've described some of the philosophy that lies behind Word IA and taken you through the installation process step by step. As far as actually using it goes, it's enough for now to know that you are really dealing with a marriage of two Windows applications, and therefore you have two distinct views of your work to get used to.

Now we'll move on to the nitty-gritty of Word IA in use. In true pedagogic style, we'll bring to life a practical task that we can all do together, learning as we go. We'll dive right in and start to create our first Web page. How do you think *we* found out how to use Word IA effectively? By trying it out, of course!

2

Your First Home Page

As every writer knows, staring at the blank page is the hardest part of writing. Your head was full of wonderful ideas before you sat down at the keyboard. Now that you're here with the blank screen in front of you, they've all flown out the window.

Before you can start your home page, you have to decide what to put on it. Unfortunately, we can't help you with that. Whaddya think we are, mind readers? Tell you what we're going to do. We're going to pretend we work for the public relations department of a small company that thinks big and wants to get on the Web. The World Wide Widget Corporation (WWW Corp. for short) has been making widgets for the large machinery business for about 200 years. The company wants to expand its sales, but has a small advertising budget and can't afford to hire many new sales representatives right now. However, WWW Corp. does a pretty brisk business over its 800 number. After all, just about any machine larger than a bread box uses their widgets.

A young whippersnapper who works for the company (the president's grandson, in fact) has come up with the idea of using the Web to advertise its products and 800 number, and maybe even to take orders. After all, a lot of the regular clients already have e-mail. He thinks the company might be able to serve its customers faster, increase its market and, who knows, maybe even expand the international business. The president has given this the green light, and we've been told to come up with a design for a Web site and suggest how we might turn some of the company documents and brochures into Web pages.

In this chapter, we'll use Word IA to create a home page for the World Wide Widget Corporation. *Home page* is Web-speak for the first page that viewers will access when they visit our site. We'll add to this with some other pages in Chapter 4, and then in Chapter 6, we'll turn some existing documents into Web format. But before we start designing our home page, let's look at how a typical Web page is made.

Deciding What to Put on Your Home Page

Web documents are called pages because physically they look a lot like pages you might find in a magazine. The magazine analogy is, in fact, a useful way of looking at Web pages. Your home page is like the table of contents in the magazine. This is the page that announces who you are and tells your readers what's available for reading. Instead of turning pages to get to individual articles, you click on a hyperlink that will take you to the article you want.

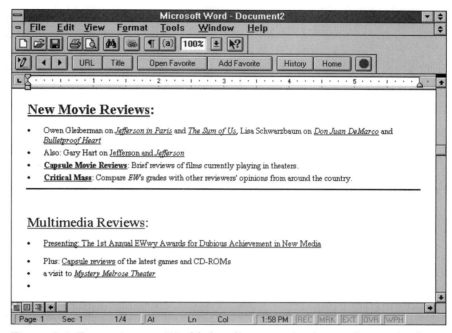

Figure 2-1: Entertainment Weekly's *online magazine is a good example of an initial home page which serves as a table of contents.*

Most home pages have a short statement of purpose—a little company blurb, personal statement or an announcement telling you what this Web site is about. Then there's a list of services, information documents and related resources accessible by hyperlink. Finally, they'll tell you who sponsored or wrote this page and where you can get in touch with them—usually an e-mail address, but perhaps also a "snail mail" address and telephone number. This home page is usually just the starting point for your Web site visitors, but it's an important front for you. If you want to trap flies in your Web, you've got to make it attractive.

Assuming you've got information to distribute, the place for that is going to be in separate Web documents you'll link to this home page. There's a good reason for this: Web pages with a lot of decoration—a nice, colorful company logo, and maybe a picture or two and designer buttons to click on—usually take a bit of time to download. You don't want your potential readers to get impatient and leave before you even get to show them your stuff. So serving up information in controlled page-size pieces is good design. A 20,000-word brochure with 50 illustrations may look great, but nobody will stick around to see it.

Weaving Your Own Web

When you start to create a Web site, it helps to realize that you are yourself weaving a small Web in your own little corner of the Web universe. The files that you mesh together by hyperlinks are the components of your Web.

So starting with our home page, we'll branch out into several documents with different types of information, designed to suit the various uses of our site. But just as it's worthwhile to think first about what types of documents we're going to post and who's going to read them, it's also useful to decide in advance where we're going to post them. We'll be creating hyperlinks in our documents as we go, and we don't want to remake all those links later because documents have ended up in different places.

Word IA lets you publish documents in two ways. The first and obvious way, which we've already discussed, is on a server connected to the World Wide Web, which means that the whole world of computers can connect to your site. But hypertext can also be a very useful and easy way for people to share information on a local network. In effect, you create a private Web accessible only to those on your in-house network. Figure 2-2 shows a possible use of this kind of private Web.

How you set up your directory structure depends very much on how you intend to publish your information. In the next section, we'll discuss a recommended directory structure for documents destined for publishing on the World Wide Web. If you plan to publish on a local web, see the instructions in the sidebar "Publishing on a Local Web."

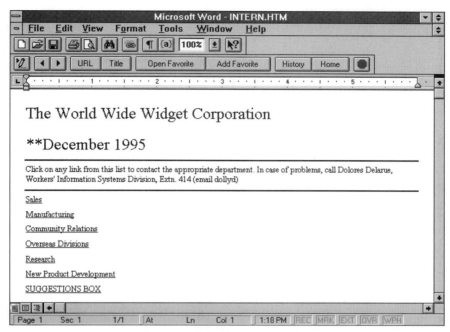

Figure 2-2: *Company information can easily be shared in-house through a local web with hypertext links.*

Setting Up Your Web Directory

You can imagine that our Web site will easily end up with six to ten documents or more that will be linked together. Embedded in each of these will be graphics: a company logo, decorative buttons and rules, some tables and graphs and maybe a few pretty pictures (like one of our new plant). Some of these graphics may be used in more than one document. We'll probably reuse our company logo regularly, and if we decide to have a red rule, for instance, we may want to use it on all our documents as a design element. These graphics won't change much, unlike some of our documents. It makes sense to put all our graphics in one directory, so we can easily call one up at any time by browsing that directory.

What we're working toward is a prefab construction that we can pick up as a piece and post on the Web, such that everything stays in the same relation with everything else. We want all the hyperlinks to work the same way they did on our own computer. The way to accomplish this is to set up a directory structure for our files that we can then transfer onto the Web. To do this:

1. Create a main directory called c:\web. Your home page (which we'll create in the next section) goes into this directory with the file name default.htm. This file will be the starting point for anyone entering your site. It should be the only file in this directory.

2. Make two subdirectories of c:\web called c:\web\pages and c:\web\images.

3. In c:\web\pages, put all the documents that you intend to create links to. (These needn't yet be in HTML format— we'll take care of that later.) Any new documents you create will also go here.

4. Save all graphics in the \images subdirectory. If you already have a company logo, say, or pictures in digital format that you've used in newsletters or brochures, you can put them here. If you don't have any, don't worry. We'll round those up later.

5. When you're ready to post your site on the Web, you'll use the MS-DOS command XCOPY C:\WEB /S [destination], where [destination] is a directory on the Web server analogous to the main directory you called c:\web on your local drive. The hyperlinks among your documents should work the same on the Web server as they did on your local drive.

Of course, we won't be ready for step 5 for awhile. But now that you've got everything set up, you can start to create your first Web document.

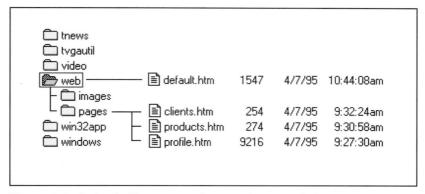

Figure 2-3: *A simple file structure for your future Web site.*

Publishing on a Local Web
When publishing on a local network, many of the documents you'll want to link to may reside on different drives throughout the network. For instance, you'll go to one place for reports from the sales department, another for information from the manufacturing plant and another for the research division. You don't need to assemble these in one place on one drive. You only need to know where they are so you can make the proper links when you're ready.

- **Make sure all the documents you want to link to are saved and in their final locations on the local web.**

- **Open a new document using the HTML template. Save the document on the network drive in its final location on the local web. *Do not save it to your local c: drive*. If you do, the links you create won't work for anyone but you.**

- **When you create links to documents on other network drives, an Unable to Create Relative Link dialog box will appear. The links you are creating *will be valid on the local web*, so choose Continue and create the link as you intended.**

We'll go over this last point again when we create hyperlinks later in this chapter, but it's important to understand the difference right now between links you create on a local web through a network and those you create on your own computer for posting on the World Wide Web.

Starting Your Web Document

Starting your first Web page is as easy as beginning a Word document—because that's exactly what you do. Open Word and choose New from the File menu. From the Template drop-down list, choose Html (Figure 2-4). This is the new template (html.dot) that Word IA added to your template files for creating HTML documents. This is no ordinary template, however. As soon as you choose it, the toolbar displays a few different options. Don't worry about them right now. We'll explain them all in detail as you need them and in Chapter 3, "The Edit View." For now, let's just get going.

Figure 2-4: *To start an HTML document, choose the Html template from the Template list.*

First, of course, you'll want a title for your document. Since that's the first item on the page, let's choose a Heading level 1 for that. From the Style drop-down list in the Formatting toolbar, choose Heading 1 (H1), then type in a title. It could be "Mrs. McCreary's Third Grade Class Project" or "My CD Collection," but in our example it's just "The World Wide Widget Corporation." (Later we'll replace this with the company logo, but we haven't figured out how to do that yet, so we'll settle for this plain-Jane version.)

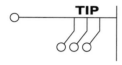

TIP

You can also choose Style from the Format pull-down menu to apply your heading and other formatting options. However, the font choices that are previewed in the Style dialog box will apply to your screen only, since the format options for HTML documents do not include a choice of fonts.

You'll notice when you click on the Style list that there are actually six heading levels available in HTML (see Figure 2-5). You'll also notice, if you've been using Word a lot previously, that you have no choice of font or size—in fact, that option has been removed from the toolbar. Font and size are not under your control when you make a Web page. It's the individual Web browser that controls the look of a page, including what typeface and font size to use. Some browsers even allow users to partially customize the look of their screens to their taste. While this may frustrate your design intentions at first, it actually makes your job as a Web author easier. And it's important to keep in mind so you don't waste time creating graphical elements no one will ever see.

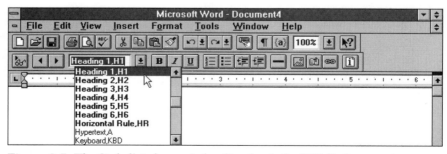

Figure 2-5: *The Style list shows six heading levels for HTML documents.*

Now, to provide a little subtitle to let people know what we're all about, we're going to add a second-level head, "Suppliers of Widgets, Gizmos and Thingamabobs." We'll give that an H2 heading and save our work as default.htm.

Wait! Not so fast! Saving your document in the proper format is trickier than it may seem, and just a little deceptive. If you use the Save option on the File menu you must change the File Type at the bottom of the dialog box to HyperText Markup Language before saving (see Figure 2-6). A better option is to choose the Save As option from the File menu because the File Type will default to HyperText Markup Language (HTML), in accordance with the HTML template you are using. You can then simply type default.htm in for the file name and choose OK.

From now on, Word will know that this is a HTML file and will bring up the appropriate editing screen whenever we call up the file. Note that when you start a new Word session and reopen your document from the HTML Edit screen, you must select All Files in the dialog box if you want to see your .htm files displayed. If you open a document from the Web Browse screen, .htm files will be displayed as well as .doc files.

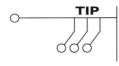
TIP

It's not enough to just add the .htm extension to your document. If you use the Save option and do not change the File Type box to HyperText Markup Language (HTML), Word will save the document as a Word document by default. When you next open it, it will look like a valid HTML document because you will have the HTML template and editing screen, but it will not work as an HTML document.

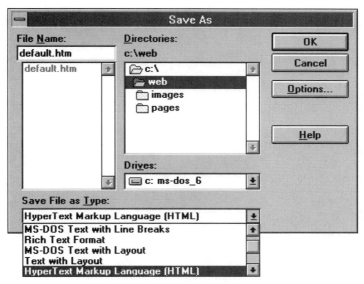

Figure 2-6: *Be sure to choose the HTML file type when you save your file.*

Adding Paragraphs

Now it's time to put some information on the page. Bearing in mind that this is just a sort of cover page and table of contents for our Web site, we're going to make it short and sweet—just a paragraph of management-approved prose saying what we're all about. We choose Normal,P from the Style list and type in the blurb that appears in Figure 2-7.

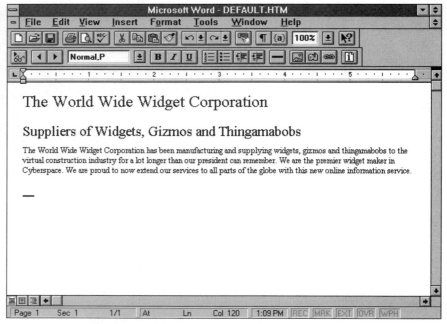

Figure 2-7: *Our Web page is beginning to develop.*

Of course, just as in a Word document, you can type paragraph after paragraph using the default paragraph style, and each time you press Enter you'll get a new paragraph. Gee, this is easy!

Naturally, if you already have some material in text format, whether on Word or another Windows text processor, you can Copy and Paste from that document using the Edit commands.

Adding a List

Now let's put in three introductory menu items. We haven't yet created the documents we're going to link to here, but it's part of the grand plan that we want to be able to show when the boss next checks our progress.

To make these menu items clear as choices, we'll make a bulleted list out of them. We could just as easily make them a numbered list—the procedure is the same, and no different than you use with Word documents, except that Word IA inserts HTML codes behind the scenes.

We can choose List Bullet,UL from the Style list first (see Figure 2-8), then type our three items; the bullets will be automatically supplied as we go. Or we can type our three items, block them and then convert them to a bulleted list by choosing List Bullet,UL from the Style list or by clicking on the Bulleted List button on the toolbar.

For a numbered list, choose List Number,OL from the Style list or click the Numbered List button on the toolbar. Word IA supplies the numbers just as it does the bullets.

KEYBOARD TIP *If your mouse finger is getting tired, use the keyboard command Alt+O/B for a bulleted list and Alt+O/N for a numbered list, using the Format pull-down menu (see Figure 2-9).*

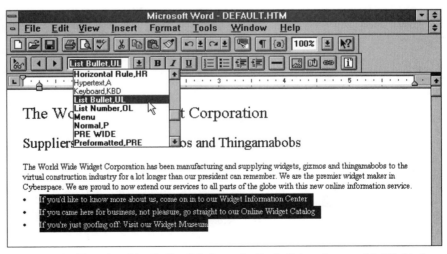

Figure 2-8: *Choosing List Bullet,UL from the Style list makes our highlighted text into a bulleted list.*

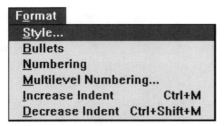

Figure 2-9: *You can choose Bullets or Numbering from the Format menu for a list.*

Adding Rules

Rules—horizontal bars—are used a lot in Web page design. The reason is simple: Not only do they make a page look smarter, but they also help define areas of information or create page-like separators in a long document.

If you browse the Web at all, you can't help but notice all the variations there are on horizontal rules: there are red bars and green bars and blue bars and even bars of rainbow hues. There are rules that look like musical staffs and rules that look like fuses leading from live bombs. All of these fancier examples are actually pictures in Graphics Interchange Format, commonly referred to as GIFs. We'll talk more about how to use these in Chapter 4, "Using Images & Links Creatively." For now, we're just going to add a few rules as separators in our page, since we haven't learned enough yet to play with graphics. Also, as a matter of principle, it's a good idea to rough out the content of the page before getting fancy.

Let's decide where we want our horizontal rules. One between the subtitle and our introductory blurb would be nice. Create a new line there by pressing Enter, then scroll down the Style drop-down list and click on Horizontal Rule, HR. You can do this even more easily using the Rule button on the toolbar. To try it, position your cursor after the bulleted list and click on the Rule button. This will place a rule before the next main section of text, as you can see in Figure 2-13.

KEYBOARD TIP *The keyboard command Alt+I/R also accomplishes this neatly using the Insert menu pull-down (see Figure 2-10).*

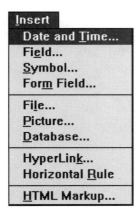

Figure 2-10: *You can insert a hyperlink or a horizontal rule from the Insert menu.*

Creating Hyperlinks

So far this document looks no different than any other you might create using Word, and maybe even a little plainer than most. However, now it's time to get around to what HTML is all about. We're going to create some hyperlinks. The key to our hyperlinks will be the "anchors." An anchor is text that will appear highlighted in blue in our document and will allow anyone who clicks on it to travel off to other destinations we have in mind for them.

We have three documents in mind. One is "Our Company," a nice little glossy brochure that tells people who we are and what we do. The second is a more mundane document, "Our Products and Services." The third is "Our Customers." Just to get the layout clear, let's type in these three items on separate lines first, bearing in mind that the words we choose will be the hyperlink anchors. (See Figure 2-11.)

To create a hyperlink:

1. Save your file first. (If you haven't done this previously, be sure to save it as an HTML file.) Valid hyperlinks cannot be created in a file that has not been saved or has been edited since the last save.

2. If you've typed in your link text already, block the text you want to become your anchor. If you have not typed in the text, just position your cursor where you want the link to appear.

3. Click on the Hyperlink button. The Hyperlink dialog box appears (see Figure 2-11). Choose the To Local Document tab.

4. Either enter your anchor text in the Text to Display box, or edit the text you've already blocked (which appears automatically in this box).

5. Browse the directories to choose the document you wish to link to, or type in the File Name. If you're writing for later Web posting and followed the instructions earlier in this chapter, this will be a file in your c:\web\pages directory. If you're writing for a local web, choose Network to go to other drives where the documents you want to link to are located.

6. Click on OK. Your hyperlink will be created.

KEYBOARD TIP   *To create a hyperlink, you can also use the keyboard command Alt+I/K through the Insert pull-down menu (Figure 2-10).*

After you've entered your hyperlink information and chosen OK, the Unable to Create Relative Link box may appear (see Figure 2-12). If it does, you may or may not have reason to be concerned. The reasons this may appear are:

≫ If you're creating a hyperlink from your document to a document on a different network drive, the Unable to Create Relative Link dialog box will appear regardless of what you do. The link you are creating *will* be valid on a local web, so simply choose Continue and the link will be created as you intended. Remember, though, that all your linked documents must reside on their final network drives, and not on your local c: drive. You can disable this message in the future by checking the Don't Show This Message Again box in the warning dialog box.

◈ If you're not on a network, chances are you haven't saved your file. Go back to Step 1 and start over. If you have saved your file and are sure everything is hunky-dory, choose Continue (and hope this bug gets worked out in future).

If you're having trouble making your links without the Unable to Create Relative Link dialog box popping up, or they don't look as you think they should, you can safely go ahead for now. You'll be able to edit your links later on. We'll show you how in Chapter 4, "Using Images & Links Creatively."

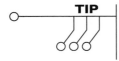

TIP

If you try to create a link from a document on a network drive to a document on your local c: drive, your link will not be valid. The link will work for you, but not for anyone else on the network.

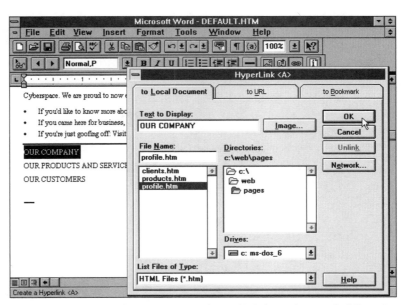

Figure 2-11: *We're about to create a hyperlink from the words "Our Company" to the document profile.htm.*

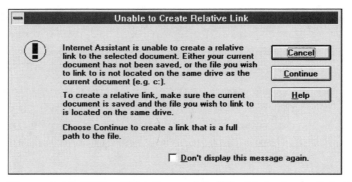

Figure 2-12: *If Word IA tells you it is "Unable to Create Relative Link," you'll have to check your work carefully.*

Testing Your Links in Web Browse View

Now that your links are in place, you're probably anxious to find out how they work—and of course it's a good (but not infallible) test of whether you did it right.

If you've gotten overanxious and tried to click on your highlighted links already, you may have discovered it doesn't work right away the way you think it should. Clicking once on your hypertext highlights the whole anchor. Double-click to go to the linked document. (When you get a mouse pointer, rather than a cursor, you know it's working.) Alternately, you can go to the Web Browse screen and your hyperlinks will work with a single click (a better choice if your mouse skills aren't that great or your mouse is not very sensitive).

So far you've been working only in HTML Edit View. To switch to Word IA's Web Browse View, click on the little eyeglasses icon on your toolbar. Then watch what happens.

The first thing you'll notice is that the toolbar has changed. You now have a whole new set of options, appropriate not for editing, but for Web browsing. Your page still looks the same—but wait a minute! What's happened to the mouse pointer? Instead of getting an editing cursor over the document screen, you now have a mouse pointer arrow on the screen, as you normally get when you point to toolbar items.

So go ahead. Poke one of your links. Did it work? If it did, and your link was to an HTML document, you're still in Web Browse View with the new document on your screen. Click the Go Back arrow on the toolbar to return to your original document.

If your link was to a non-Word document (or a Word document without the typical .doc extension), a package icon appears on your screen to indicate an embedded object. Double-click on the icon to open the document in HTML Edit View, or click the right mouse button to see options. To return to your original document, close the second document (File/Close or Alt+F/C) or change windows using the Window pull-down menu.

If your link didn't work, we're afraid you'll have to repeat the course on creating hyperlinks. Don't worry—it's probably just that your file is not where you thought it was or you overlooked some little instruction in a hurry.

TIP

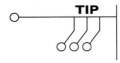

To read a non-HTML, Word document accessed via a hyperlink, the user must have either Word or a package called Word Viewer, which Microsoft makes available for non-Word users. If you want to make your Word document available to any Web browser, you must convert it to HTML. See Chapter 6 for details on how to do this.

You'll find that you can't edit your anchor text by inserting a cursor the usual way, because Word IA treats the anchor as a single item. To edit the anchor text, highlight it, then click on the Hyperlink button again (or use the Hyperlink command on the Insert menu) and edit your anchor text through the Create Hyperlink dialog box.

If you want to see what your links actually look like in hypertext, click on the Html Hidden button on the toolbar. Besides being able to look at your hypertext links, you'll be able to edit them here, once you know what you're doing. In fact, you now have an editing cursor and some limited editing options from this screen. Click on the button again, and you're back to the browsing options.

That's all we're going to do with Web Browse View for the moment. We'll come back to it for a more thorough look in Chapter 5. But for now, let's click on the pencil icon and return to the HTML Edit View. We've got a little tidying up to do on our first home page before we're finished.

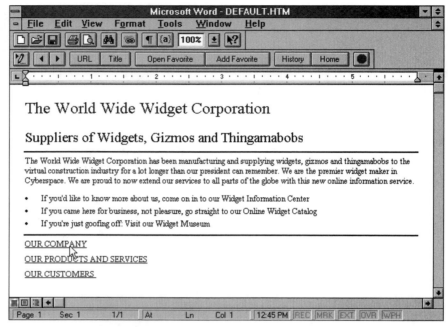

Figure 2-13: *Switch to Web Browse View to test your links.*

Signing & Titling Your Page

Often the Web seems like a three-ring circus where things are constantly changing. New pages come online every day, and there's always something novel and interesting to look at. On the other hand, some pages hang around long past their useful life, like moldy cheese in the corner of the refrigerator.

To be kind to your potential Web site visitors, and to form good habits from the beginning, it's a good idea to sign and date your page. Of course, we at the World Wide Widget Corporation want to give people a way to contact us, too. It's part of our expressed goal.

It may seem obvious when you think about it (but you'd be surprised how many people don't) that a Web address is not an e-mail address. That means that nobody will be able to e-mail us about our page or the information in it unless we give them our e-mail address here, too.

Using the Address Tag

To finish off our page neatly, let's add another rule and then put in some contact information. We'll use the Address tag on the Style list for this. This uses the Web convention of setting off address information in a special style. Netscape and Mosaic usually show the address in italics. Other browsers might display it right-justified or indented.

Choose the Address style, then enter your information. In this case, we'll use our 800 number and our "snail mail" and e-mail addresses. You can see what we've done in Figure 2-15.

Of course, design-wise, you could just as easily have entered your information in normal paragraph style, or even chosen a header style for it if you wanted. However, the Address tag makes the address easily identifiable and allows browsers to treat it in their usual fashion.

Another common use of the Address tag is to put a shorthand version of the address—such as initials or a business or personal name—at the bottom of each of a Web site's documents. This is then hyperlinked to a separate document containing more detailed information about the author, company or service responsible for the Web site.

Giving Your Document a Web Title

Finally, you'll want to give your document a Web title. Now pay attention: this can get a little confusing. This title is not something that will appear on your screen. Also, it may or may not be the same as the title you put in earlier at the top of your document—the one that *does* appear on your screen. Rather, this title is the name by which your page will be known on the Web (or on your local net, if that's where you're displaying it). It is also the name any Web indexing service will use to help people find you. So although you might be tempted to choose something witty, like "Wee Willy Widget's Home Page," you'd be better off choosing something that accurately reflects your content. This title is one of the hidden codes Word IA puts at the top of your document.

There are two ways you can title your document. The easiest, if you're a mouse-o-phile, is to click on the Title button on your toolbar. The other is to use HTML Document Info on the File pull-down menu (Alt+F/H for you keyboard jockeys), as shown in Figure 2-14. Either one brings up the box labeled HTML Document Head Information (Figure 2-15). In the space for Title, type the name you've chosen and choose OK.

Until you access your page later with Word IA or another Web browser, you won't see what you've done. But it helps to know that whatever you type in will appear in the colored title bar at the top of the screen on a Web browser—the same bar that Word uses to display the name of the file you currently have open. As proof that it's there for Web browsers to find, we'll take a look at it in the next section.

You'll be able to view the title when you are in Web Browse view by clicking on the Title button on your toolbar.

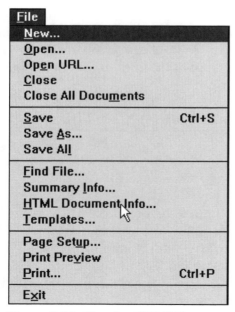

Figure 2-14: *Choosing HTML Document Info on the File pull-down menu allows us to enter information about the file that doesn't appear onscreen.*

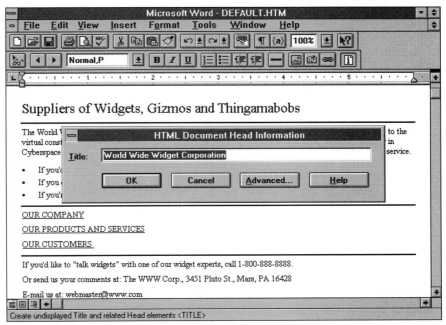

Figure 2-15: *This is the title by which other Web browsers and searchers will identify our document.*

A First Look at HTML Code

So far this hasn't been hard at all, has it? That's because what you're really doing has been hidden from you. But you might be getting curious about just what you've been doing all along. Let's take a look. Save your file and close it, being sure to save it as the HTML file type, and with the .htm extension.

Now call up the file again, using the File/Open (Ctrl+O) command. Make sure the Confirm Conversions box is checked (see Figure 2-16). Once you select a file with the .htm extension, Word gives you the Convert File dialog box with HyperText Markup Language (HTML) highlighted. This time, scroll up to Text Only, then choose OK (see Figure 2-17).

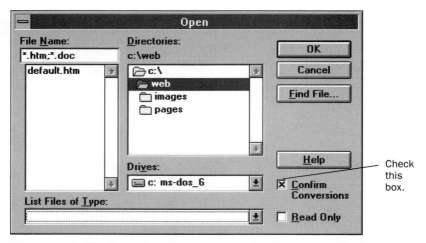

Figure 2-16: *Check Confirm Conversions so that Word IA will allow you to open your file in another format.*

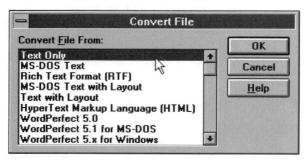

Figure 2-17: *To see our file as a text file, we change the file type to Text Only.*

What you'll see is similar to Figures 2-18 and 2-19. Notice all the HTML codes that have been added to the document for each of the commands we've learned. Did you do that? You bet your sweet bippy, you clever dog, you. Welcome to the world of Web authoring!

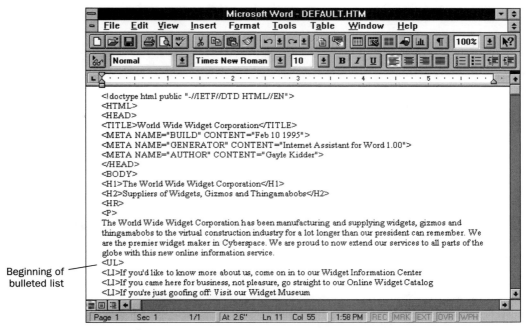

Figure 2-18: *Looking at our Web page as a text file allows us to see all the HTML tags.*

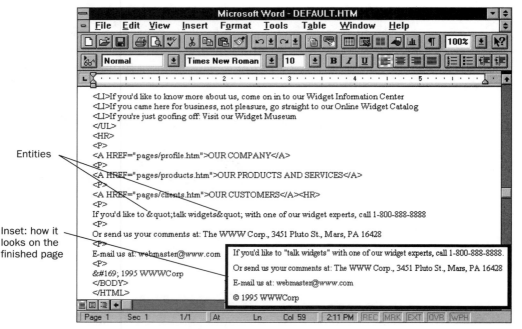

Entities

Inset: how it looks on the finished page

Figure 2-19: *Among the HTML codes in the lower half of our page are the hypertext links and "entities"—the codes HTML uses for special symbols like quotation marks and the copyright symbol.*

Help! Don't Leave Me Here!

You didn't think we were going to abandon you with an open text file, did you? Actually, we thought about it. It seemed like such a nice ending to the chapter. But conscience got the better of us.

Just close the file. You haven't done it any harm by opening it as a text file—it's still the same file. The code at the top of the file identifies it so that the next time you call it up, Word will know to ask you if you want to convert it from HTML. Choose OK to have the file back in your familiar Word format.

Moving On

In this chapter, you've learned the basics of composing a Web page. Using the simplest of HTML commands and Word IA's easy menus, you've learned how to

- set up your Web directory structure
- create headings and paragraphs
- create a bulleted or numbered list
- add horizontal rules
- create relative links among your documents
- add an HTML address and title to your document

You're probably thinking this is a piece of cake by now. In the next chapter, we'll tour the HTML Edit screen and go methodically through the toolbar buttons and menu choices you need to create Web documents.

3

The Edit View

If you decided to dive right in and follow our example in Chapter 2, you may already be the proud owner of your very own Web page. By now you should be anxious to see what else can be done with this budding Web site.

You've already become familiar with several of the toolbar buttons and previewed the dialog boxes you'll use for HTML formatting. There are more commands available both in the toolbar and the pull-down menus. Some duplicate what you've already seen, and others offer more advanced HTML options.

In this chapter, we'll review all the toolbar buttons first and then go on to the menu options. When menu commands duplicate toolbar buttons, you'll find the fullest explanation under the toolbar description, since that's usually the quickest way to accomplish your aims.

The Toolbar Buttons

When you first open an HTML file, either by opening a new file with the HTML template or by loading a preexisting HTML document, a new set of toolbar buttons appears on your screen (see Figure 3-1). Some of these, like the Hyperlink button, are entirely new to you. Others, like the List and Indent buttons, are familiar. It's important to realize, however, that these familiar buttons do not always function as they do in an ordinary Word document. In this section, we'll go over all of the new buttons first, and then go on to some familiar toolbar buttons whose usage in HTML is special.

Figure 3-1: *The toolbar: a few new buttons and some familiar ones with new uses.*

Switch to Web Browse View Button

This is the button to use when you want to see your page as it will look to a Web browser, test your hyperlinks or browse other pages on the Web. When you choose this option, Word IA actually loads another template called Webview (webview.dot), which it uses to display your current file.

You can also switch to Web Browse View using the View menu command Web Browse (Alt+V/W). When you switch to Web Browse View, the eyeglasses on the button will change to a pencil. To return to the HTML Edit screen, choose the button again or select HTML Edit from the View menu (Alt+V/E).

To browse the World Wide Web, you must first open your Internet connection. For a thorough explanation of the Web Browse screen and how to use it, see Chapter 5.

Horizontal Rule Button

Use this button to insert a horizontal rule at the point you select in your document. Note that you cannot change the width or other dimensions of this rule. The way it is displayed depends on the Web browser through which the page is viewed. If you want to use a wider rule or a colored rule, you will need to use a GIF graphic. These colored rules are widely used and available on the Web. See how to do this using the Picture toolbar button discussed in the next section.

Picture Button

Graphics are so common on Web pages that Word IA has made it really easy for you to insert them. Just click on the Picture button on the toolbar, and you're on your way.

To insert a picture into a document:

1. Place the cursor where you want the picture to appear. Then click the Picture button.

2. You'll get the Insert Picture dialog box, shown in Figure 3-2. Browse your directories to choose the graphic you want to insert, or type its name in the File Name box. If you're on a network, choose Network to browse the network drives.

3. In the Alternative Text to Use If Image Cannot Be Displayed box, type the text you want to appear when images are not displayed.

4. Choose OK, and the image will be imported to your file.

For most routine image insertion tasks, that's all there is to it. The Insert/Picture option on the File menu accomplishes the same thing with the keyboard.

Graphics must be of the .gif or .jpg type to work in both Word IA and on the Web. (See Chapter 4, "Using Images & Links Creatively," for more explanation of graphics.)

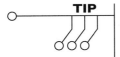

Word 6.0 users who routinely handle graphics will be used to getting resizing handles when they import a picture and click on it. Sorry! That works in Word because the picture is incorporated into the document together with all sizing and placing information. In HTML, however, the GIF file remains separate, so you must size your inline images using an independent image processing application.

If you choose Advanced from the Insert Picture dialog box, you can choose advanced options, such as how you want text on the same line to align to the picture. Word IA itself always displays text aligned to the bottom line of a picture, but it allows you to choose Top or Center. This lets the text be aligned as you specify when Web browsers that allow these options display the page.

You can use the Sensitive Map option to designate a picture as a link to several different destinations, depending on where on the map the user clicks. See Chapter 7, "Advanced HTML Options," for a discussion of sensitive maps.

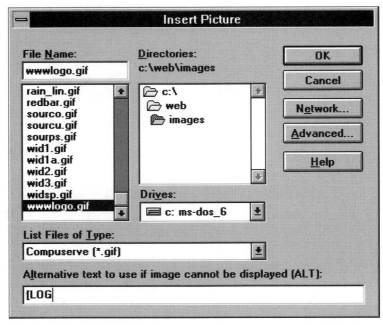

Figure 3-2: *Clicking on the Picture button brings up this dialog box, where you select the graphic to insert in your file.*

Bookmark Button

The Bookmark button inserts an internal anchor in your HTML document. You can then create a hyperlink to this point somewhere else in the same document or in another document. This makes it possible to skip easily from one section of a document to another, or from a point in one document to a designated section of another document.

While you can create bookmarks in any Word document, the added dimension of Word IA is that you can create hypertext links to your bookmarks. A bookmark may be "empty" (just a point in your document) or it may contain associated text.

Add a Bookmark

To add a new bookmark:

1. Position your cursor at the point where you want the bookmark. Or highlight a section of text you want bookmarked. Click on the Bookmark toolbar button to bring up the Bookmark dialog box (Figure 3-3).

2. In the Bookmark dialog box, you'll see a list of bookmarks in the current document. Type in the name that will serve as the identifier of your new bookmark. The name must begin with a letter and contain no spaces (you can use an underline character to substitute for a space if you like).

3. Click on Add.

You won't see the bookmark in your text, but you can prove it's there by using the Bookmark button to go to it from another point in your document.

To do this, create your bookmark first as described above. Then create the hyperlink to it by choosing the Hyperlink button (or select Hyperlink from the Insert menu and choose the Bookmark tab). For detailed instructions, see "To Bookmark" in the "Hyperlink Button" section of this chapter and "Branching Out With Links" in Chapter 4.

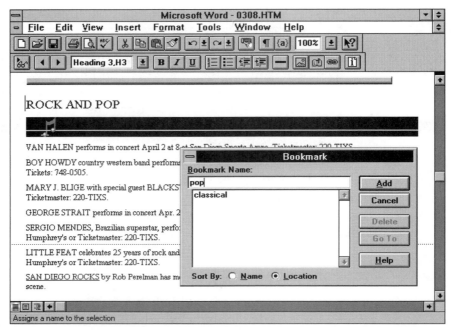

Figure 3-3: *We're creating a bookmark at the top of the Rock and Pop section of this music calendar.*

Display Bookmarks

To display your bookmarks in the text:

1. Choose Options from the Tools menu.

2. Select the View tab.

3. Under Show, select Bookmarks and then OK.

The beginning and end of a bookmark are indicated with square brackets in your document.

Find a Bookmark

To go to any bookmark in the current document:

1. Click on the Bookmark button (or choose Bookmark from the Edit menu).

2. Select the bookmark you want to go to.

3. Choose Go To. If you've chosen a section of text as your bookmark, that text will be highlighted.

By default, bookmarks are displayed in the Bookmark dialog box alphabetically. You can display them in order of location in the document by choosing the Location radio button.

Other Bookmark Options

You can edit, move, copy and delete bookmarks and any associated text:

* *Deleting a bookmark*—To delete a bookmark, select the bookmark you want to delete in the Bookmark dialog box and choose Delete. This deletes the bookmark but does not delete any selected text in your document associated with it. To delete both bookmark and text, highlight the text on your screen and use your Backspace or Delete key. You can delete just a part of the text that defines a bookmark without deleting the bookmark itself.

* *Moving a bookmark*—To change the location that a bookmark is assigned to, click on the new location or select the new text to be bookmarked. Then select Bookmark, highlight the name of the bookmark you want to change and choose Add. The bookmark will be deleted from its previous location and inserted in the new one.

* *Cutting and pasting a bookmarked item*—If you cut an entire bookmarked item and paste it in a new location in the same document, the bookmark moves with it.

* *Copying a bookmarked item*—If you copy an entire bookmarked item to a *new* document, a bookmark is created in the new document. If you copy a bookmarked item to another location within the *same* document, Word IA keeps the original bookmark. It does not create a bookmark for the copied text.

Hyperlink Button

The Hyperlink button creates a hyperlink consisting of an *anchor* and a *destination*. The anchor is the word or words to be clicked on to follow the link, and the destination is an embedded code that tells the Web browser where to go next. There are three types of links that can be created, as indicated by the tabs on the dialog box that appears when you choose this option (see Figure 3-4):

- To URL
- To Local Document
- To Bookmark

In Chapter 4, "Using Images & Links Creatively," we illustrate how to create links of all three types.

To URL

A hyperlink to a URL takes you to another document, on another computer and in another location, anywhere on the Web. That document could be at a tire factory in Akron, Ohio; a university in Oslo, Norway; a beach resort in Byron Bay, Australia; or the camel bazaar in Goulimime, Morocco—if they have a Web server. And who knows? They might.

Choosing the Anchor

The first thing you must choose, as with any hypertext link you create, is what you will use in your document as a link—the anchor. This can be

- text (a word or phrase)
- image (usually an inline .gif)
- both text and image

If you choose a text link, you can highlight the text in your document or simply choose the insertion point, then click on the Hyperlink button and type the text in the Text to Display box (see Figure 3-4).

If you want an image to serve as your anchor, you can highlight an image already in your document, then click on the Hyperlink button to proceed. Or insert the image as you create the hyperlink by choosing the Image button in the To URL dialog box. Then choose the image file you want as your anchor from the Insert Picture dialog box (see Figure 3-2 and "Picture Button" above). The image is inserted in your document at the point you chose and appears with a blue border indicating it is a hyperlink.

If you want your link to include both text and image, complete both steps.

Choosing the Destination

To finish creating your link, choose the document you want to link to in the Hyperlink dialog. This must be in the form of a complete URL (see the sidebar "Web Addresses & How to Read Them" in Chapter 1). Word IA keeps a list of the URLs you have already used, and you can select from one of these if you wish.

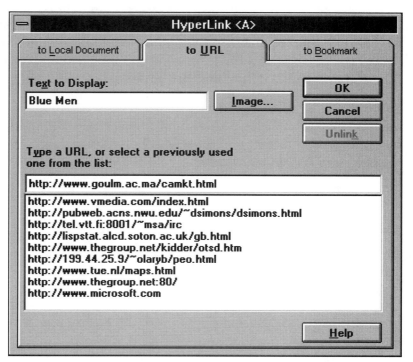

Figure 3-4: *Choose the To URL tab to create a link to another Web site.*

To Local Document

Use the To Local Document tab to create a link to a document on your own network or server site. (See Figure 3-5.) While you are creating your Web site, this document may reside on your own computer. Word IA calls this a *relative link,* since it does not require a full URL address for the document but only a location in relation to the current document.

For an illustration of creating relative links to local documents see "Creating Hyperlinks" in Chapter 2 and "Branching Out With Links" in Chapter 4. Here's a review of the procedure:

1. Save your file first.

2. Choose the text and/or image to display, as above.

3. Choose the file to link to. If you are on a network, this must be a file on a network drive, not a file on your local c: drive (or the link will only work for you).

4. Choose OK.

Word IA can be touchy about creating relative links. It likes everything to be exactly right. If everything's not exactly right, it flashes the Unable to Create Relative Links dialog box, which may or may not be a cause for concern. See Chapter 2 for further explanation if you have this problem.

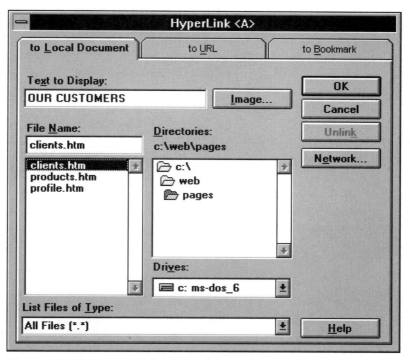

Figure 3-5: *Choose the To Local Document tab to create a link to another document at your site.*

To Bookmark

A hyperlink to a bookmark will take you to a bookmark previously created in the same document. To create a bookmark link:

1. First create the bookmark (the point you want to link to). To create your bookmark, see "Add a Bookmark."

2. Go to the point where you wish to insert your hypertext link. Select the text you wish to be your link (unless you would rather type it in—see step 4).

3. Click on the Hyperlink button (or choose Insert/ Hyperlink). Choose the To Bookmark tab. (See Figure 3-6.)

4. If you selected text for the link, it appears in the text box. If you didn't, type the text now in the Text to Display box. You may also choose to insert an image as your link (see "To URL" above).

5. From the list, choose the bookmark to link to and then choose OK.

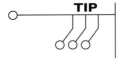 **TIP**

If you want to create a link to a bookmark in a different document, do not use the To Bookmark tab from the Hyperlink dialog box. Instead, you must create a link to the document using the To Local Document option, then edit the link. Keep reading for an explanation.

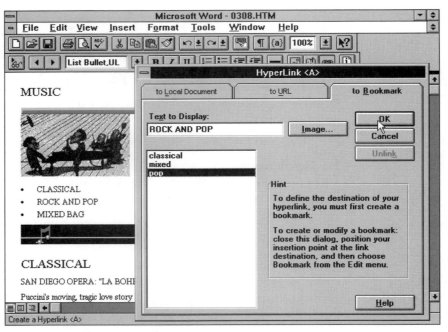

Figure 3-6: *Here we're creating a link to the bookmark we made in Figure 3-3.*

Links to a Bookmark in Another Document

At times you might want to create a link to a bookmark in another document. This is one occasion where Word IA expects you to learn a little HTML coding. Don't panic—it's easy.

A bookmark link takes the form *filename.htm#markit*, where *markit* is the name of your bookmark.

We'll use the name Document 1 for the document you're linking *from* and the name Document 2 for the document-with-bookmark that you're linking *to*. To create this link:

1. First create the bookmark in Document 2. To create your bookmark, see "Add a Bookmark."

2. Go to the point in Document 1 where you wish to insert your hyperlink. Select your anchor text and click on the Hyperlink button (or choose Insert/Hyperlink).

3. Choose the To Local Document tab and create your link to Document 2. (See "To Local Document" above.)

4. Now click on the Html Hidden {a} button. In the code that is revealed, find the link to Document 2 you created and position your cursor immediately after the file name.

5. Type **#*markit*** after the file name, where *markit* is your bookmark name.

See Chapter 4, "Using Images & Links Creatively," for an example of using bookmark links.

It goes without saying (but we'll say it anyway) that you can't create your own bookmark link to a point in a document posted by someone else on the Web, because you can't edit that person's page to insert your bookmark. But if a bookmark already exists and you are able to find it by displaying the code of that Web page, you can use it as a link destination. To do this, you would have to make a link to the URL including the bookmark as above. The full link address would then read, for example: **http://www.microsoft.com/default.htm#bookmark**.

Of course, since the destination document is not under your control, you run the risk that a bookmark may disappear without warning, making your link invalid.

Title Button

The Title button creates the title by which Web browsers and searchers will identify your document. This title does not appear on your screen, but is part of the information Word IA stores about your document for Web browsers to access. In most Web browsers, this title will appear in the bar at the top of the screen (the same bar that Word uses to display the name of the file you currently have open on your screen).

You enter the title in the Html Document Head Information dialog box that appears when you click on this button (see Figure 2-15). There are some more advanced options you can choose from this dialog, which are discussed in Chapter 8, "Tips & Tricks."

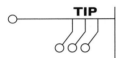

TIP

Many Web searchers use the title of your document as a key to content. Therefore, if you want your page to be referenced properly, be sure that your title accurately reflects its content.

Html Hidden Button

Use this button to reveal hidden HTML codes on your page. Doing so lets you see information about your hyperlinks and embedded images. You can edit these links once they are revealed.

By no means are all HTML codes revealed with this option. If you want to see and edit all of your HTML codes, first close your file and then reopen it as a text file:

1. Choose the File/Open option. In the Open dialog box, check Confirm Conversions before selecting the file you want to open. Choose OK.

2. In the Convert File dialog box that comes up next, change the file type to Text Only, then choose OK. (See Figure 2-17.)

For more on editing your file as a text file, see "Editing Your Links" in Chapter 4, and see Chapter 8, "Tips & Tricks."

Numbered List

Bulleted List

Increase Indent

Decrease Indent

List & Indent Buttons

You can create a numbered or bulleted list using the appropriate toolbar buttons (or the Format menu commands), just as you use them in Word. HTML codes for creating a list will be inserted in your document.

The Increase Indent buttons and Decrease Indent buttons have a special function in Word IA, however. They are used to create nested lists only, like these:

- Fruit
    - Apples
    - Oranges
    - Bananas
- Vegetables
    - Green beans
    - Broccoli
    - Brussels sprouts

To create a nested list, first create your list items. Then apply the Bulleted List or Numbered List style by blocking the list text and clicking on the appropriate list button. Next, block the items you want as a second-level list and use the Increase Indent button to indent these items one more level. See Figure 3-7 for an example.

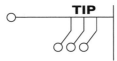

TIP

You can also create a bulleted list within a numbered list, or vice versa, using the List buttons to apply the style you want to your nested list.

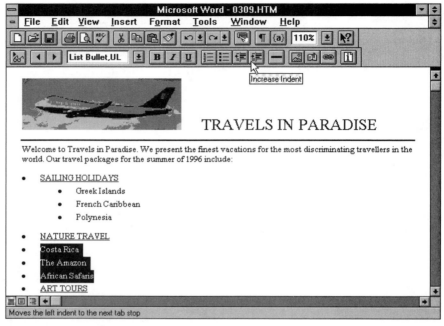

Figure 3-7: *Use the Increase Indent button to create a nested list.*

The Decrease Indent button acts as an undo command on nested lists you have created. Both indent buttons work only on paragraphs formatted with the List Number,OL or List Bullet,UL style.

HTML does not recognize indents other than those created using the List commands. If you create indented paragraphs or items using either the toolbar buttons or the Format menu commands, they will not be preserved when you save your document.

There are three other options for creating lists that are not available with the toolbar buttons, but can be called up using the Style feature: the menu list, directory list and definition list.

Menu List

A menu list is virtually identical to a bulleted (or unordered) list in Word IA. Some browsers display a menu list exactly like a bulleted (or unordered) list. Others display it in the same indented list format but without bullets.

You create a menu list much as you do a bulleted or numbered list. Type the items to be included on separate lines. Then block the list and apply the Menu style, either from the Style drop-down list or using the Format/Style command.

Directory List

A directory list is useful for saving space when you're displaying a list of short items. Word IA displays directory list items arrayed in equally spaced rows across the page, much as if you had created three rows using tabs. (See Figure 3-8.) This can be very useful for presenting a compact page, but be aware that not all browsers will display them this way. Some treat a directory list just as they do a menu or unordered list.

To create a directory list, type the items to be included on separate lines. Each item should be no more than about 20 characters long. Then block the list and apply the Directory, DIR style, either from the Style drop-down list or using the Format/Style command. You will not see the results until you close your file and then reopen it.

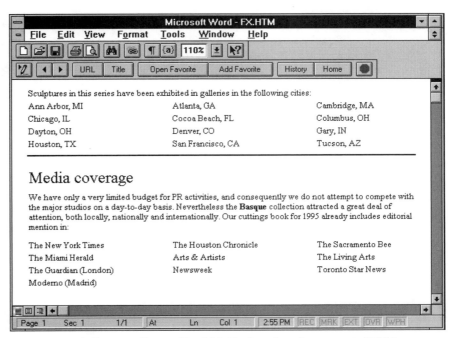

Figure 3-8: *A directory list as Word IA displays it, a feature not all Web browsers recognize.*

Definition List

A definition list is a more elaborate use of the list option for longer entries. It allows a list term to be followed by an indented paragraph, which may be as long as you like.

A definition list is created through the Style command on the Format menu. To create a definition list:

1. Type the first term in your list, followed by a Tab, and then type the definition (the explanatory paragraph) you want to follow it. When you have finished, press Enter. Repeat this step for all the definitions in your list.

2. Highlight the paragraphs you created in the steps above.

3. From the Style drop-down list, choose Definition List,DL or Definition Compact,DLC. (Or use the Format/Style option and choose one of these styles in the Styles dialog.) Then choose Apply. Definition Compact presents your text more compactly and is useful for a long list that might be easier to read that way.

You will not see how your list looks until you save, close and reopen your document. Even then, it will not look exactly as it does under a Web browser. (See Figure 3-9.)

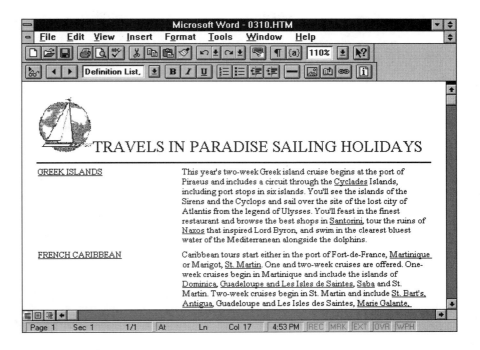

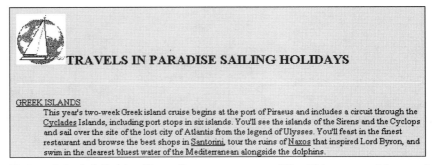

Figure 3-9: *A definition list as it appears on your Word IA screen, at top, and on the Netscape Web browser, at bottom.*

Other Word Buttons in HTML

Other toolbar buttons that you are familiar with on your Word screen also have their uses in HTML editing. The Bold, Italic and Underline buttons all produce their desired effects as they do in non-HTML Word documents. These are a few of the styles that HTML recognizes and translates to its own codes.

Changes to the Pull-down Menus

We've already seen, in passing, some of the pull-down menu options that are specific to HTML editing. Now it's time to go through the menus more systematically, seeing which new features the Internet Assistant adds to the familiar Word menus and which it removes because they have no meaning on the Web.

File Menu

Figure 3-10 shows, from left to right, how the File pull-down menu changes from the Word standard when Word IA is installed, and then again when an HTML document is actually loaded.

New... Ctrl+N	New... Ctrl+N	New...
Open... Ctrl+F12	Open... Ctrl+F12	Open...
Close	Browse Web	Open URL...
Save Ctrl+S	Close	Close
Save As...	Save Ctrl+S	Close All Documents
Save All	Save As...	Save Ctrl+S
Find File...	Save All	Save As...
Summary Info...	Find File...	Save All
Templates...	Summary Info...	Find File...
Page Setup...	Templates...	Summary Info...
Print Preview	Page Setup...	HTML Document Info...
Print... Ctrl+P	Print Preview	Templates...
Exit	Print... Ctrl+P	Page Setup...
	Exit	Print Preview
		Print... Ctrl+P
		Exit

Figure 3-10: *The File menu sequence.*

As we mentioned back in Chapter 1, immediately when you install Word IA the Browse Web option appears. If you choose it, Word IA switches you to the Web Browse screen and loads default.doc—a fine starting point and general introduction to the Web.

Once you are working on an HTML document, as indicated in the rightmost panel of Figure 3-10, that option is replaced by Open URL. A URL, as you'll recall from our venture to the London Natural History Museum in Chapter 1, is the universally recognized address of a Web page. Unless you are working at a server site, this menu option will get you nowhere until your SLIP or PPP connection to the Internet has been established. If it has, you get a generously wide dialog box in which you can enter any valid URL in the world. Word IA will then switch you to Web Browse view and load that page. Once it's loaded, you are free to switch back to HTML Edit View and do what you like with it (no matter what the copyright attorneys might wish).

The only other special item on the File menu is HTML Document Info. This brings up exactly the same dialog box as does the Title toolbar button, and is merely an alternative way of titling your page (the keyboard alternative is Alt+F/H).

Edit Menu

The Edit menu acquires just one extra option—Copy Hyperlink. (See Figure 3-11.) Taking this option (keyboard Alt+E/H) places the HTML identity of the *current* page—its title and its file specification—on the Clipboard. You can then drop that into any *other* HTML page to create an instant link back to the original page. In HTML authoring, it's extremely common, at the foot of each subsidiary page in a family of documents, to set up a link so that users can return to the main page. This edit feature makes doing that a breeze.

Can't Undo	Ctrl+Z		Can't Undo	Ctrl+Z
Repeat Copy	Ctrl+Y		Repeat Typing	Ctrl+Y
			Copy HyperLink	
Cut	Ctrl+X		Cut	Ctrl+X
Copy	Ctrl+C		Copy	Ctrl+C
Paste	Ctrl+V		Paste	Ctrl+V
Paste Special...			Paste Special...	
Clear	Delete		Clear	Delete
Select All	Ctrl+A		Select All	Ctrl+A
Find...	Ctrl+F		Find...	Ctrl+F
Replace...	Ctrl+H		Replace...	Ctrl+H
Go To...	Ctrl+G		Go To...	Ctrl+G
AutoText...			AutoText...	
Bookmark...			Bookmark...	
Links...			Object	
Object				

Figure 3-11: *One extra item on the Edit menu.*

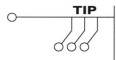

The Bookmark option on the Edit menu is not a new feature, because bookmarks are used in conventional Word documents. However, bookmarks take on added significance in HTML in creating hypertext links. For a full discussion, see "Bookmark Button" earlier in this chapter.

View Menu

As you install Word IA, the View pull-down menu acquires a Web Browse option. Easily confused with the Browse Web option on the File menu, this one simply switches you to the Web Browse screen without loading anything. In other words, it does exactly what the little eyeglasses toolbar button does.

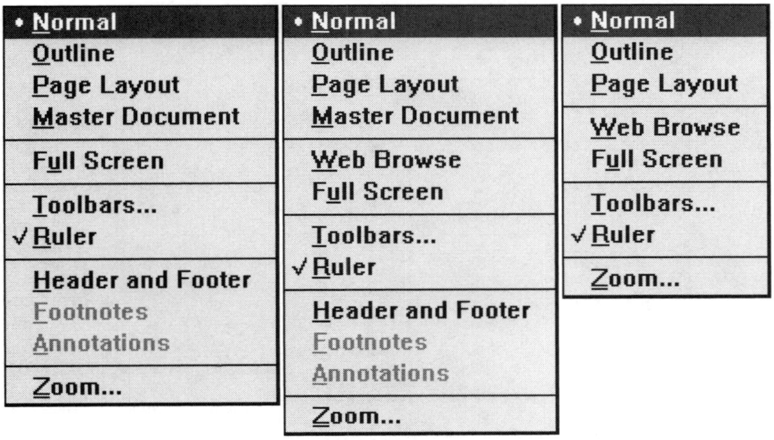

• Normal	• Normal	• Normal
Outline	Outline	Outline
Page Layout	Page Layout	Page Layout
Master Document	Master Document	
		Web Browse
Full Screen	Web Browse	Full Screen
	Full Screen	
Toolbars...		Toolbars...
√ Ruler	Toolbars...	√ Ruler
	√ Ruler	
Header and Footer		Zoom...
Footnotes	Header and Footer	
Annotations	Footnotes	
	Annotations	
Zoom...		
	Zoom...	

Figure 3-12: *Evolution of the View menu.*

This menu is more interesting for what it sheds as it evolves (see Figure 3-12). Headers, footnotes and annotations are not supported on the Web—at least not yet.

Insert Menu

There are plenty more formatting elements that lose their meaning on the Web, too. Page numbers, captions, cross references, indexes and drawing objects all disappear from the Insert menu, as Figure 3-13 depicts. Elements like files, symbols and databases are still valid in this new environment, so they stay. Two new elements, the hyperlink and the horizontal rule, just do what their equivalent toolbar buttons do.

Break...	Break...	Date and Time...
Page Numbers...	Page Numbers...	Field...
Annotation	Annotation	Symbol...
Date and Time...	Date and Time...	Form Field...
Field...	Field...	
Symbol...	Symbol...	File...
Form Field...	Form Field...	Picture...
		Database...
Footnote...	Footnote...	
Caption...	Caption...	HyperLink...
Cross-reference...	Cross-reference...	Horizontal Rule
Index and Tables...	Index and Tables...	
		HTML Markup...
File...	File...	
Frame	Frame	
Picture...	Picture...	
Object...	Object...	
Database...	Database...	
	HyperLink...	

Figure 3-13: *The Insert menu loses a few items.*

HTML Entities

Word for Windows is extremely good with symbols, making it possible to write about déjà vu or the £/¥ exchange rate with relative ease. HTML, being international, allows for a full range of accented letters but they usually have to be specially coded by hand—quite a chore, especially if you're Swedish. Using Word IA, you just insert symbols normally and the software takes care of converting them to so-called HTML "entities." Here's what a few accented letters end up looking like in the source code:

é   é

ü   ü

Å   Å

Now a few surprising ones, necessary because the characters they represent have special meanings in HTML:

<	&lt;
>	&gt;
&	&amp;
"	&quot;

...and finally,   means a nonbreaking space.

All of the HTML entities can also be written in numerical form (&169; means the copyright symbol, and so on). For a complete list in both formats, see Appendix C.

That leaves one final, interesting new option: HTML Markup (Alt+I/H by keyboard). "Surely," we hear you exclaim, "HTML markup is what this entire enterprise is about: How can it also be a mere afterthought of a menu option?" The answer is that the designers of this software wisely recognized that HTML is a rapidly evolving language, and that the range of formatting options offered by their menus and buttons can't possibly keep up as new tags are internationally accepted, not to mention the informal ones sure to find their way into the HTML vernacular. If you click on this option, then, you will be presented with the dialog box shown in Figure 3-14, which allows you to enter manually any tag you like, on the basis of "on your own head be it—we don't guarantee this is going to work."

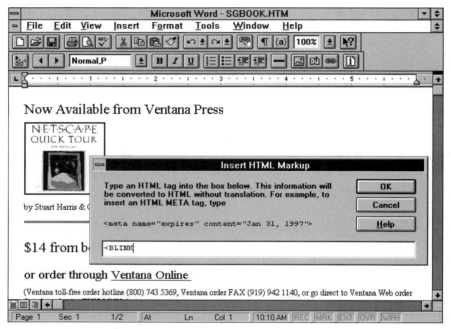

Figure 3-14: *Entering the <BLINK> HTML tag manually.*

Figure 3-14 catches us in the act of entering a particularly controversial tag—the <BLINK> tag that makes everything between it and a </BLINK> tag flash on and off. This style is meaningful *only* in the Netscape browser, and many Internet gurus find it offensive, not only because blinking screens make them feel bilious but also because Netscape Communications Corporation implemented this gimmick without waiting for agreement by all other interested parties. Tut, tut.... Figure 3-15 shows the disdain Word IA has for this vulgarity, and we have much more to say about this controversy in Chapter 8, "Tips & Tricks."

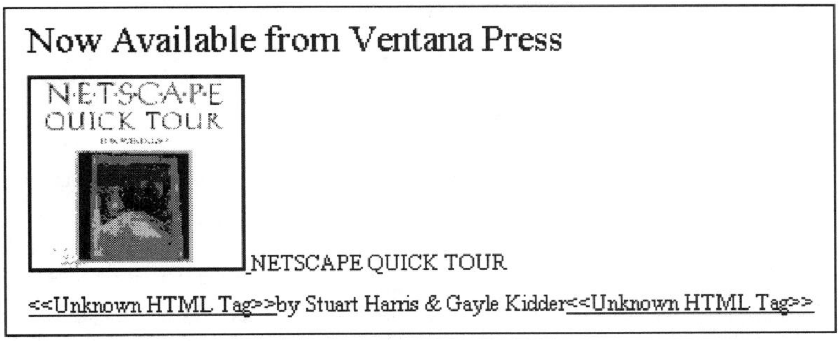

Now Available from Ventana Press

N·E·T·S·C·A·P·E
QUICK TOUR

NETSCAPE QUICK TOUR

<<Unknown HTML Tag>>by Stuart Harris & Gayle Kidder<<Unknown HTML Tag>>

Figure 3-15: *Word IA does not wish to know about blinking text!*

Format Menu

The menu that suffers most of all as Word 6.0 is converted into an HTML editor is the Format menu. Columns, drop caps and tabs are just a few of the style elements that fall by the wayside, as we see in Figure 3-16. Bulleting and numbering of lists survives (repeating the toolbar options), as do indentations, although they have limited use in HTML. They can only be reliably applied to previously formatted lists in order to create nested lists (see the explanation under "List & Indent Buttons" earlier in this chapter).

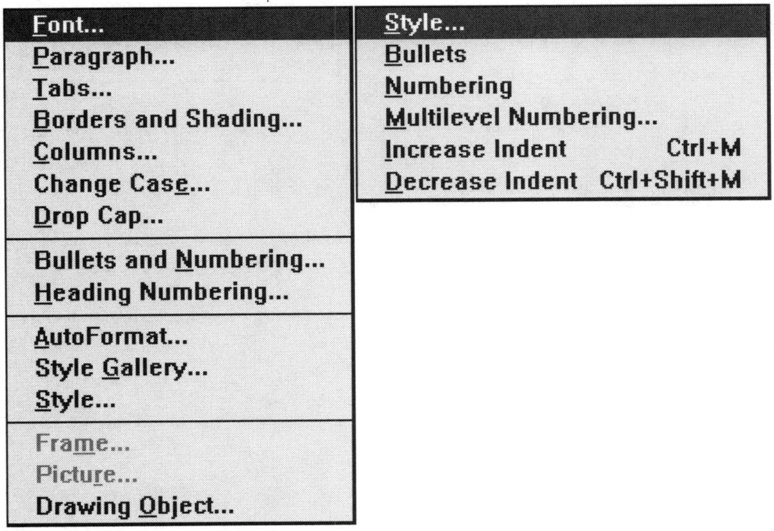

Font...	Style...
Paragraph...	Bullets
Tabs...	Numbering
Borders and Shading...	Multilevel Numbering...
Columns...	Increase Indent Ctrl+M
Change Case...	Decrease Indent Ctrl+Shift+M
Drop Cap...	
Bullets and Numbering...	
Heading Numbering...	
AutoFormat...	
Style Gallery...	
Style...	
Frame...	
Picture...	
Drawing Object...	

Figure 3-16: *The incredible shrinking Format menu.*

Many format elements are packaged under the rubric of style here, and permit you to choose, for example, fonts to correspond with your various header levels. You should clearly understand, though, that these design choices have local application only: They absolutely do not guarantee the look of your page to somebody browsing it from South Africa or Stockholm.

Tools & Help Menus

Figures 3-17 and 3-18 show further losses and gains in the menu department, which should require no explanation. We'll end this section with a handy reference to all of the HTML Edit screen menus. Figure 3-19 shows the main menu bar, artificially stretched to fit them all side by side.

Spelling... F7	Spelling... F7
Grammar...	Grammar...
Thesaurus... Shift+F7	Thesaurus... Shift+F7
Hyphenation...	Hyphenation...
Language...	Language...
Word Count...	Word Count...
AutoCorrect...	AutoCorrect...
Mail Merge...	Macro...
Envelopes and Labels...	Customize...
Protect Document...	Options...
Revisions...	
Macro...	
Customize...	
Options...	

Figure 3-17: *The Tools menu loses four items...*

Contents	Internet Assistant for Word Help
Search for Help on...	Contents
Index	Search for Help on...
	Index
Quick Preview	
Examples and Demos	Quick Preview
Tip of the Day...	Examples and Demos
	Tip of the Day...
WordPerfect Help...	
Technical Support	WordPerfect Help...
	Technical Support
About Microsoft Word...	
	About Microsoft Word...
	About Internet Assistant for Word...

Figure 3-18: *...and the Help menu gains two.*

File	Edit	View	Insert
New...	Can't Undo Ctrl+Z	• Normal	Date and Time...
Open...	Repeat Typing Ctrl+Y	Outline	Field...
Open URL...	Copy HyperLink	Page Layout	Symbol...
Close		Web Browse	Form Field...
Close All Documents	Cut Ctrl+X	Full Screen	
	Copy Ctrl+C		File...
Save Ctrl+S	Paste Ctrl+V	Toolbars...	Picture...
Save As...	Paste Special...	√ Ruler	Database...
Save All	Clear Delete	Zoom...	
	Select All Ctrl+A		HyperLink...
Find File...			Horizontal Rule
Summary Info...	Find... Ctrl+F		
HTML Document Info...	Replace... Ctrl+H		HTML Markup...
Templates...	Go To... Ctrl+G		
	AutoText...		
Page Setup...	Bookmark...		
Print Preview	Object		
Print... Ctrl+P			
Exit			

Format	Tools	Window	Help
Style...	Spelling... F7	New Window	Internet Assistant for Word Help
Bullets	Grammar...	Arrange All	Contents
Numbering	Thesaurus... Shift+F7	Split	Search for Help on...
Multilevel Numbering...	Hyphenation...		Index
Increase Indent Ctrl+M	Language...	1 DEFAULT.DOC	
Decrease Indent Ctrl+Shift+M	Word Count...	2 NAVIGAT.DOC	Quick Preview
		√ 3 WID1.HTM	Examples and Demos
	AutoCorrect...		Tip of the Day...
	Macro...		WordPerfect Help...
	Customize...		Technical Support
	Options...		
			About Microsoft Word...
			About Internet Assistant for Word

Figure 3-19: *All the HTML Edit screen menus.*

The Style List

If you followed along and created your first Web page in Chapter 2, you've already seen the Style list in action. As a Word user, you're probably pretty familiar with the usual options that your templates give you from the Style list. But you may have noticed a few new ones that don't make a lot of sense just yet.

In fact, you may never use some of the items on the Word IA Style list. RestartList, for instance, is one you'll never need, and it's not a valid HTML tag at all. If you were to put it in, you wouldn't see it when you opened your file as a text file. It's there for Word to use in translating its own codes to HTML.

Table 3-1 lists the styles on the Word IA Style list and the effects they are intended to produce when displayed by a Web browser:

Style Name	Description
Address	Tells Web browsers to use their standard style of displaying an "address" (usually of the Web author or sponsor of the page). Often, as in Word IA, this is in italics.
Blockquote	Creates an indented block paragraph.
CITE	Denotes a citation, usually displayed in italics.
CODE	Marks text as an example of typed code, usually displayed in a fixed-width typewriter (monospaced) font.
Default Paragraph Font	Applies normal paragraph style, same as Normal, P.
Definition Compact, DLC and Definition List,DL	Used for a list of items followed by indented paragraphs that are explanatory in nature. The Definition Term, DT and Definition, DFN tags are applied automatically when you select a definition list style for your text. See "Definition List" earlier in this chapter.
Directory,DIR	Creates a directory list. See "Directory List" earlier in this chapter.

Style Name	Description
Heading,H1 through H6	Designates heading level styles at six levels. Heading font styles are under the control of the Web browser used. You can choose heading styles for your own display, but they will apply to your screen only.
Horizontal Rule,HR	Creates a horizontal rule as a divider across the screen. Can also be applied with the Horizontal Rule button or Insert/Horizontal Rule.
Hypertext,A	Indicates a hypertext link. This is inserted automatically when you create a link (do not insert manually). You can see it as part of your hypertext tag when you use the Html Hidden button to see the text of your links.
Keyboard,KBD	Marks text as keyboard input (such as might be used in manuals), usually displayed in a monospaced font.
List Bullet,UL	Creates an unordered (bulleted) list, same as the Bulleted List button.
List Bullet,NL	Creates a numbered list, same as the Numbered List button.
Menu	Creates a menu list, which may be either bulleted or plain, depending on the Web browser. See "Menu List" earlier in this chapter.
Normal,P	Denotes ordinary paragraph style.
PRE WIDE and Preformatted,PRE	Used when you want to display text exactly as typed. Text is not formatted in HTML styles, but appears as entered in a monospaced font, including spaces, which are not normally respected.
RestartList	Used by Word IA to translate certain actions from HTML to Word. (You may notice these codes appearing after horizontal rules, but they are transitory; they do not exist in your HTML text.)
Sample,SAMP	Marks text as a sequence of literal or sample characters, usually displayed in a monospaced font. →

Style Name	Description
Strong,STRONG	Displays text with extra emphasis, as defined by the Web browser, usually in bold. Same as the Bold button.
Typewriter,TT	Displays text in a monospaced font, rather than the normal paragraph font.
Variable,VAR	Marks text as a variable name, such as might be used in formulas or equations, usually displayed in italics or bold italics (Word IA uses bold italics).
z-Bottom of Form and z-Top of Form	These are automatically applied when you create a form to define the form limits. Do not attempt to insert these styles manually. See Chapter 7, "Advanced HTML Options," on creating forms.
z-HTML Tag	Inserted automatically to denote HTML code. Do not attempt to insert this manually.

Table 3-1: *Word IA styles.*

Moving On

If you actually sat down and read through this chapter beginning to end (and we suspect most of you didn't), your head may be spinning now. We've tried to thoroughly explain all the options on your HTML Edit screen. You won't have absorbed everything here all at once, of course, but this chapter can serve as a reference as you try out new things and become more skilled at Web page design.

In the next chapter, we'll return to actual page development, showing you by example how to use some of the different styles covered in this chapter. As we elaborate on the home page we created in Chapter 2, you'll learn how to use graphics in various ways and branch out into some other types of documents. Then we'll take a look at different ways to link documents as we begin to weave a more complicated web.

4

Using Images & Links Creatively

Now that we've had a good look at the commands available to us for creating Web pages, let's start using them. By now you understand that images and links each come in several types. Both are the very essence of the Web, and using them creatively will enhance your Web page designs.

We're going back to the public relations department at the World Wide Widget Corporation first to see how things are getting on.

Adding a Logo

Habitual users of Word for Windows won't be amazed at the ease with which illustrations can be brought into HTML documents— they're used to it. But Word IA's HTML Editing toolbar goes one more step in the direction of making this edit function a no-brainer: it provides a button that practically does it for you. We both tend to be "left-brained" when it comes to absorbing information, so we're frequently flummoxed by icons and pictograms. But even we have to admit that the mini-sketch of a sunrise behind a mountain is not hard to interpret as "Picture." (On second thought, maybe it's a lump of dirt being thrown on a pile—but it's worth 1,000 words, anyway.)

We'll use that feature right away to enhance the WWWidget Corporation's home page, inserting the company logo and then one of those fancy horizontal rules we've mentioned before. First, let's place the cursor where we want the picture to appear—at the extreme upper left of the document, where the logo belongs. Now hit that "pile of dirt" button, and we get the Insert Picture dialog box shown in Figure 4-1. In the figure, we've already browsed our web/images subdirectory to find the file wwwlogo.gif, and we're in the process of entering **[LOGO]** in the Alternative Text to Use If Image Cannot Be Displayed box.

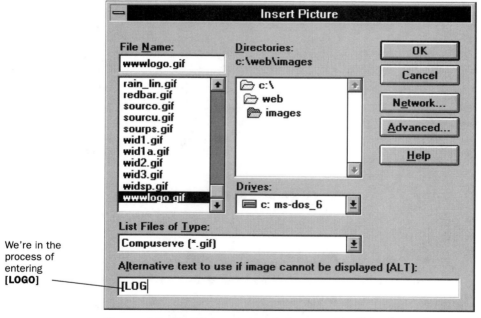

We're in the process of entering **[LOGO]**

Figure 4-1: *The Picture button brings up this dialog box, where we choose the graphic file that contains our logo.*

What's the point of that? A good Web designer always remembers that not all visitors to a site see its images. Some users deliberately turn off the image-display functions of their Web software to benefit from faster loading. And there are still many thousands who use the Lynx browser, a UNIX application that displays text only. For those users, the alternative text, or *ALT* text, as it is known, offers a clue about the content of the missing pictorial. It's particularly useful for those with image-display off, who might decide to view certain individual images on the basis of what the ALT text promises. Who could resist the WWWidget corporate logo?

We'll be explaining a few more imaging options later, but for most routine image-insertion tasks, that's all there is to it. Just OK that dialog box, then delete the normal horizontal rule by placing the (tiny) cursor at its left end and hitting the Delete key. We have built up quite a collection of fancy rulers and, going through exactly the same Image Insert routine, we decide on one called rain_lin.gif. Having done that, Figure 4-2 shows what our page now looks like. To see rain_lin.gif in its full Technicolor glory, turn to the gatefold in the back cover of this book. Figure 4-3 shows how a Mosaic user with images turned off would see the same screen.

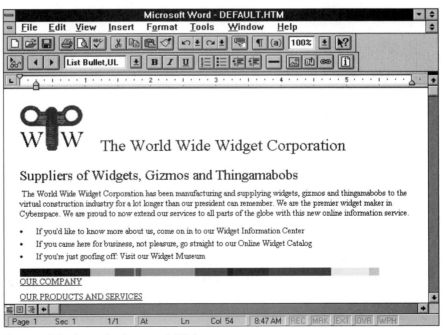

Figure 4-2: *A newly decorated Widget screen.*

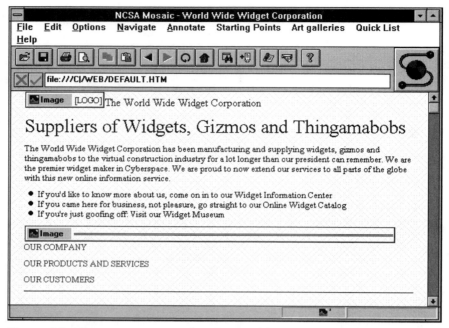

Figure 4-3: *The same screen seen by Mosaic with images turned off, showing the importance of the ALT text.*

Images as Links

Well, in our imaginary corporation we've made a little headway by now. Having attended six meetings and made 11 "presentations" to important people in varying states of alertness, somebody has apparently decided that the WWWidget Corporation will forge onward into the future. Even our department of audio-visual aids (hitherto consisting of one arthritic ex-journalist jealously guarding a VCR and a set of crayons) has been made over for the purpose. We now have a far better set of crayons, computer image manipulation software, and a scanner that will make data files in TIFF, GIF or JPEG format out of anything you lay on it (and the less said about that unfortunate experiment after the annual office party, the better).

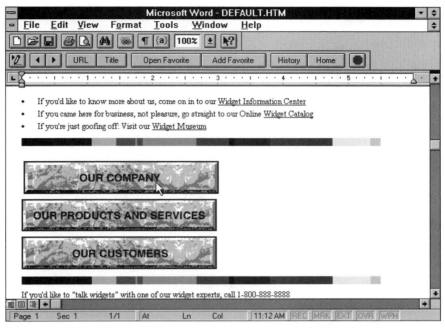

Figure 4-4: *Marble slabs as hyperlink buttons.*

The benefits of the new resources are clear in Figure 4-4: a jazzed-up version of Figure 2-17. We did it by blocking the original link anchor words, then hitting that Hyperlink toolbar button and deleting the anchor text in the dialog box. Then we used the Image button in the same box to call up one of the marble slab pictures, done in GIF format. The hyperlink destinations remain exactly the same, and each slab is outlined in blue as a visual cue that it's an anchor.

Links to Images & Other Media

Notice that the Widget Information Center, the Widget Catalog and the Widget Museum also now have links. The president really liked our idea for the Widget Museum (although our boss, the heir apparent, took credit for it). He even gave us some pictures from his office wall to use.

Figure 4-5 is part of the Widget Museum, and Figure 4-6 shows what you get when you click on the anchor to the Great Widget Mill. Yes, the destination of a hyperlink can be something other than a document—it can be a movie, a sound byte or a bigger picture. Since this picture is external rather than *inline* (see the sidebar ".GIF, .TIFF & .JPEG"), it can be in JPEG format, which generally gives better resolution than GIF but takes longer to load.

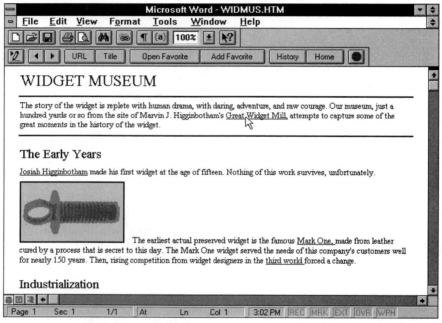

Figure 4-5: *A section of our Widget Museum...*

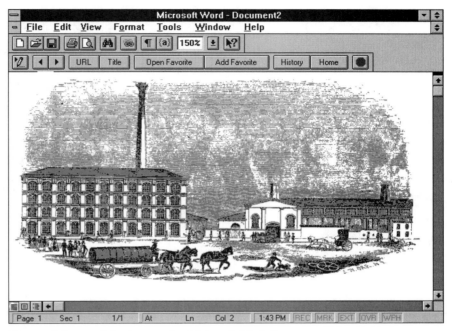

Figure 4-6: *...and the impressive history behind it.*

.GIF, .TIFF & .JPEG

Those alphabet-soup file extensions all refer to different ways of encoding a picture for storage as an ordinary computer data file. The granddaddy of them all is TIFF (.tiff or .tif)—the Tagged Image File Format, which creates humongous files. Many other formats, including the very popular GIF (Graphics Interchange Format), were invented in an attempt to compress the data more effectively. A few years ago, an expert committee called the Joint Photographic Experts Group (JPEG) thrashed out a new format that was supposed to supplant all others and become an industry standard. Hence the JPEG (.jpg or .jpeg) format, which has so far failed to become the standard but may nevertheless be the best.

It's generally true to say GIF is the most compact format, but JPEG offers better quality in the end. GIF is the format invariably used to create all the little thumbnail images that decorate Web pages. In this case, data compression is more important than quality. Because they are really considered part of the document (even though you can choose not to see them by turning off image mode), they're known as inline images. JPEG files are more frequently used as external images, referenced by a link—either hypertext or a smaller GIF file turned into a link. The user can then decide whether to take the time to download them.

Advanced Image Options

Take another look at Figure 4-1, the Insert Picture dialog box—or, if you prefer, hit that "pile of dirt" button and bring it up on your own screen. See that Advanced button? If you select it, Word IA brings up yet another dialog box—the one shown in Figure 4-7.

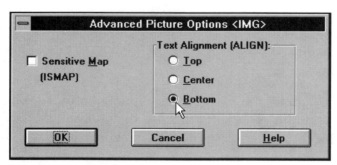

Figure 4-7: *Advanced picture options.*

Notice those three radio buttons for Text Alignment—Top, Center and Bottom? Text Alignment is an attribute you can give to your inline pictures that determines how the picture will line up with any text that you place on the same line, such as captioning text.

But there's a snag here. Word IA's screens are constrained to follow the standards of Word 6.0 in the matter of text/picture relationships, so they will always display pictures *as though their Text Alignment attributes were Bottom,* regardless of how you set those radio buttons. Word IA (like most browsers) displays as much text as will fit on a line next to the picture and wraps the rest below the picture. If you want only a part of text next to the picture, simply enter a hard return after that part to insert a paragraph break. If you want a line break without the extra spacing that is created with a paragraph, you have to use the Insert/ Html Markup option and enter the HTML tag <BR>. You won't see this until you close and reopen your file. (See Chapter 8, "Tips & Tricks," for more on inserting HTML tags not on your menus.)

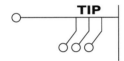

TIP

Note that you can also choose a heading style for text placed next to a picture, as shown in Figure 4-8.

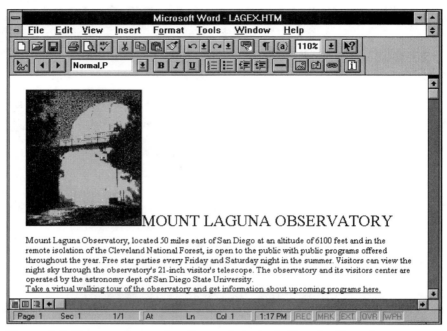

Figure 4-8: *You can choose a heading style for text aligned with an image.*

To check any page design that involves a Text Alignment attribute other than Bottom, you need an independent Web browser. We recommend that you get and install Netscape or Mosaic and use it to check your page design. (Of the two, Netscape supports more display options—it can even display a paragraph aligned to the left or right of a graphic, although Word IA does not yet allow you to create this type of alignment. See Figure 4-9 for an example of this.)

The last option in the Advanced Picture Options dialog, Sensitive Map, will be explained in Chapter 7, "Advanced HTML Options."

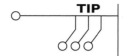

When inserting images, always bear in mind the time it will take to download the image from the Web. Remember that accessing an image from the Web can take three or four times as long (or even longer) as it does to load from your own computer, depending mainly on the user's modem speed and browser. A good rule of thumb is that an image will take approximately a second per kilobyte for the average user to download. (A 65kb image will thus load in about a minute.)

Branching Out With Links

Organizing your material with links in mind is critical to making information accessible to your readers. Links provide an easy way for readers to find just the information they want, without having to read through a lot of stuff they're not interested in. Remember also that keeping your files small will make them easier to use as they'll load a lot faster.

Using hyperlinks in Web authoring can be quite a creative process, once you get the hang of it. You needn't feel limited to using hyperlinks just for a menu of choices. They can be used quite freely to bring any text to life in new ways.

The arts and entertainment calendar home page shown in Figure 4-9 illustrates several different uses of hyperlinks. Note the way they've been used in the leading text paragraph. The links go straight to the events cited by means of bookmarks inserted in other files.

This Web site is, in fact, composed of 15 different files, linked together in various ways. We refer to that collection as a *family* of files, because if you mapped out the relationships among the files it would look a bit like a family tree. There are also several links to URLs at other Web sites.

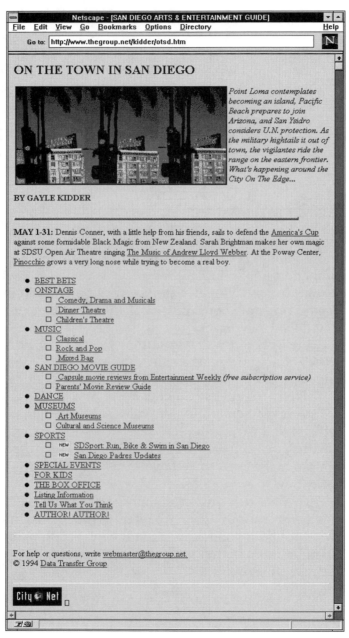

Figure 4-9: *This arts and entertainment calendar home page illustrates several types of links.*

One of the great benefits of Web publishing is the way it allows you to offer information in a number of ways without taking up more resources (such as paper!). The "Best Bets" and "For Kids" sections of this calendar, for instance, are simply culled from items in the other files and presented in a way that makes them readily accessible.

In the following section, we'll demonstrate the different types of links in this calendar as we show you how to create links among a family of documents.

Using Bookmarks as Links

As a general rule in Web design, breaking things down into several small files is better than offering just a few big ones. But sometimes there's good reason to keep a larger file together for readers who want to peruse an entire topic. It can be irritating, after all, to be confronted with a multiple-choice questionnaire every few paragraphs. If you want to print out information from a Web page, the process can become laborious, too, when everything's in different files. Bookmarks can be just the key to pleasing all tastes.

Note that visitors to the Web site in Figure 4-9 can choose to go straight to the "Rock and Pop" section of the music file if all they want is quick information about a rock concert this weekend and don't feel like wading through opera and symphony concerts.

In Chapter 3, "The Edit View," we used this same file, music.htm, to illustrate creating a bookmark link within a file (see Figure 4-10). Now we'll create the links from our home page to the bookmarks in the music.htm file.

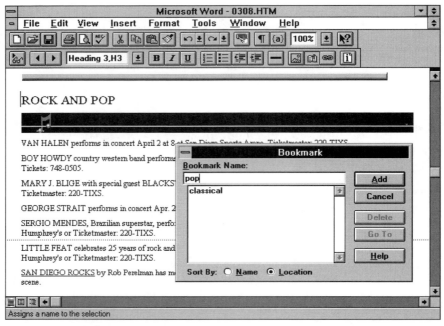

Figure 4-10: *We're inserting a bookmark in this section of our music.htm file, which we'll then make a link to.*

This is how to go about making links to bookmarks in a different file, using the Music links in this calendar as an example:

1. First, create the text from which the links will originate. In our example, this is the list of main topics on the arts and entertainment home page shown in Figure 4-9. Next, highlight a topic and use the Hyperlink button to link it to your destination file. (In our example, we made "Music" link to the file music.htm.)

2. Open the destination file—the file you want to insert bookmarks into (e.g., our music.htm file). At the beginning of each section you want to link to, use the Bookmark button to insert a bookmark and give it a relevant name (e.g., "classical" or "pop"). See Figure 4-10 above. This name will not appear on the finished page, so it needn't be the same as the anchor text, but it is the name you'll use in creating your link.

Increase Indent

3. Go back to the original file. Under each topic, enter a list of subtopics that will link to the bookmarks you just created in the destination file. (In our example, we entered **Classical, Rock and Roll** and **Mixed Bag** under Music.) Make it into a nested list—that is, block the list and click the Increase Indent button. Call the subtopics anything you like; their names need not match the bookmark names.

4. Highlight a subtopic and choose the Hyperlink button to turn it into a link to the destination file. Use the Local Document tab (*not* the Bookmark tab) to do this, and insert the name of your file (i.e., music.htm). See Figure 4-11.

5. Click on the Html Hidden {a} button. Insert your cursor just after the file name in the link information and type ***#bookmark***, where *bookmark* is the name of the bookmark you want to link to (in our example, classical). See Figure 4-12 to see how this looks in our file.

6. Click on the Html Hidden button again to make the code disappear.

7. Repeat steps 4 through 7 for each subtopic.

Now your links should work exactly as you intend. Double-click on a link to check it out. Alternatively, switch to Web Browse View and then click once on the link to follow it. (If your mouse is not very sensitive, you may find this easier from the Web Browse screen.) You should find the link taking you straight to your bookmark.

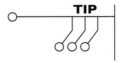

TIP

Once you've created a link to a bookmark in another file, you'll find that you can't delete or change your hyperlinks using the Hyperlink button (it no longer brings up the Hyperlink dialog box). Use the Html Hidden button to reveal the codes, then insert a cursor to edit your links.

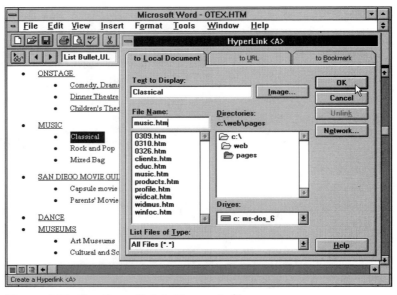

Figure 4-11: *Creating a link to the music file.*

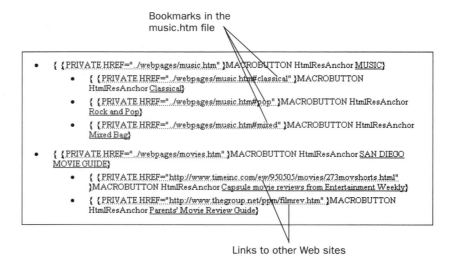

Figure 4-12: *With hidden HTML codes revealed, inserting the bookmark names makes these links go to the right points in the music.htm file.*

Links to Other Web Sites

So far all of the links we've created have been to other documents within our own little web. However, every link is a doorway to a new adventure, and linking to other sites on the Web can add a new dimension and excitement to your pages. And it's so easy that it would be churlish not to offer your readers the thrill.

Take another look at our Web page in Figure 4-9 and you'll see a few uses we've made of this kind of link. We thought it would be a nice service to make movie reviews available to people who might come to our pages. We don't offer movie reviews ourselves, but we know a few Web sites that do. Both Capsule movie reviews from *Entertainment Weekly* and *Parents' Movie Review Guide* are hyperlinks to other Web sites. You can see the full URLs of these sites in Figure 4-12.

You can create external links in one of two ways:

❧ *If you know the URL of the address you want to link to*—Simply create your link using the Hyperlink button (or the Insert/ Hyperlink menu command). Choose the To URL tab, select the text to display as your link text and type in the full URL of the site you want to link to. (See Figure 4-13.)

❧ *If you find a page you want to link to while in Web Browse View*—You can create a link to any Web document while it's on your screen by using the Copy Hyperlink button or the Edit/Copy Hyperlink menu option. The title of the document and its URL will be put on the Clipboard. Use Edit/Paste to copy it into any other document as an active link.

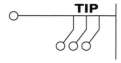

TIP

Most Web page authors are delighted to have other authors link to their pages. The more links, the more possible ways for people to find their sites. However, when dealing with copyright material, you should be mindful of legal considerations. If in doubt, a quick e-mail message asking permission to include the link would be wise as well as polite.

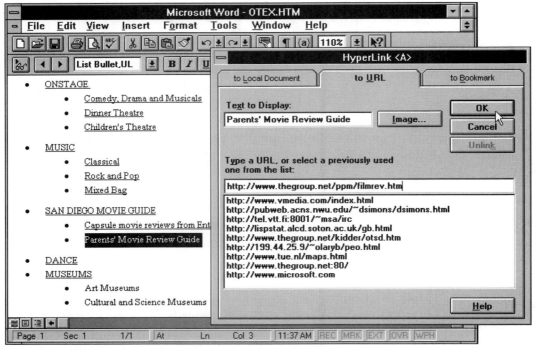

Figure 4-13: *Creating a link to another Web site.*

Editing Your Links

Despite your best intentions, sometimes links won't turn out just the way you want. And sometimes things just change. A URL changes, or a file moves to a new drive on your local network or you decide to rearrange your bookmarks.

It's also possible you've been working on your local computer on a network and now want to post your files on the network or Web. In order to do so, you'll have to change the links to reflect their new status.

In Chapter 2, "Your First Home Page," we told you not to worry if you couldn't get your links to look as they should—we'd show you how to fix it later. Well, as the Walrus said, the time has come.

The Way of All Links

Let's start with a primer on how your links should look. In Figure 4-14, you'll see examples of all the link types described below.

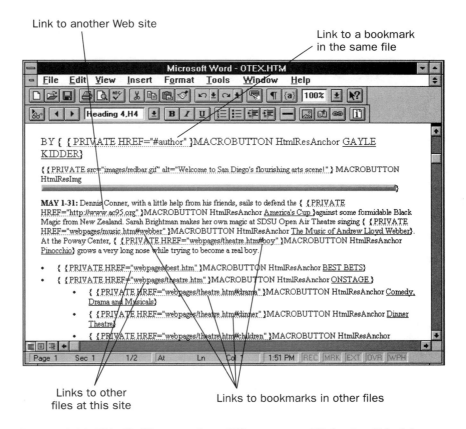

Figure 4-14: *This file illustrates how different types of links should look in your Word IA file.*

Links to URLs

Links to URLs will have this format in the HTML source file:

```
<A HREF="http://www.ac95.org">anchor text</A>
```

When the hypertext links are revealed with the Html Hidden {a} button in Word IA, the same address will look like this:

{ {PRIVATE HREF="http://www.ac95.org"} MACROBUTTON HtmlResAnchor America's Cup}

Links to Bookmarks: Same File

Links to a bookmark within the same file will have this format in the HTML source file:

<A HREF="#author">anchor text</A>

which looks like this in Word IA:

{ {PRIVATE HREF="#author"} MACROBUTTON HtmlResAnchor I. M. Author}

Links to Files

Links to a file will vary slightly according to the destination file's location relative to the original file.

- If the file is within the same directory, the link will look like this in the HTML source file:

    <A HREF="music.htm">anchor text</A>

    and like this in Word IA:

    { {PRIVATE HREF="music.htm"} MACROBUTTON HtmlResAnchor Music}

- If the file is in a subdirectory of the current directory it will look like this in an HTML source file:

    <A HREF="webpages/music.htm">anchor text</A>

    and like this in Word IA:

    { {PRIVATE HREF="webpages/music.htm"} MACROBUTTON HtmlResAnchor Music}

- If the file is in a different subdirectory, it will look like this in an HTML source file:

    <A HREF="../webpages/music.htm">anchor text</A>

    and like this in Word IA:

    { {PRIVATE HREF="../webpages/music.htm"} MACROBUTTON HtmlResAnchor Music}

Links to Bookmarks: Different File

Links to a bookmark in a different file combine the above two formats and look like this in the source file:

```
<A HREF="webpages/music.htm#classical">anchor text
</A>
```

In Word IA, the same address will look like this:

```
{ {PRIVATE HREF="webpages/music.htm#classical"}
MACROBUTTON HtmlResAnchor Classical}
```

Links to Network Files

Links to files on a network take this appearance:

```
<A HREF="F:/sales.htm">anchor text</A>
```

In Word IA, the same address will look like this:

```
{ {"LOCAL:F:/sales.htm"} MACROBUTTON HtmlResAnchor
Sales Department}
```

Mind Your Syntax!

One of the most critical and easily overlooked things about all of the above examples is that the actual links are encased with quotation marks. If the quotation marks are missing (perhaps because you edited the hyperlink and accidentally deleted them), the links won't work, unless you have an extremely forgiving Web browser.

Editing your links is a relatively easy thing to do. Just click on the Html Hidden {a} button to reveal your links. If you discover you've got the URL address wrong in your link, just slip your cursor in at the appropriate point and edit it.

If your bookmark link to another file isn't working, take a look at the link and see if you deleted the end quotation marks when entering your bookmark. Insert the cursor in place and put the quotation marks back.

If you got those constant, irritating Unable to Create Relative Link messages when you made your hyperlinks and chose to ignore them and continue, chances are your links look like those in the network example above instead of like relative links to local files. (There may be a *c:* before the file name.) To make them work on the Web, you'll have to edit them before posting. Simply put your cursor in and edit out the drive letter and colon if it's not appropriate. If all your links are like this, you can fix them with a simple Find-and-Replace operation.

Once you've edited your links, remember to save your file before trying them again.

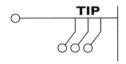

TIP

When making links to other Web sites or editing your links manually, bear in mind that you must enter a URL exactly, matching the URL's use of upper- and lowercase (you'll find them overwhelmingly lowercase, but the few exceptions need to be respected). HTML tags will work in either upper- or lowercase, but the machines that serve up your document are often very fussy.

Moving On

If you've been using the examples in this chapter to develop your own Web pages, they're probably taking on a lot more sophistication by now, and you should be feeling pretty chuffed. In this chapter, you've learned the various ways to use images in your files, and you've seen hyperlinks in action. It's beginning to seem that this Web page business isn't as complicated as you first thought.

Now it's time to take a look at the other side of Internet Assistant for Word—the Web Browse View. We've already peeked at this a few times as it became necessary to check the links we created. But there are a lot of other things you can do with it, including visiting other places on the Web. In the next chapter, we'll look at the Web Browse View and show how to use it to open up the world of the Web.

5

The Web Browse View

So far we haven't seen much of Word IA's other screen—the Web Browse View. You may have discovered that it's more convenient to check links you're making from this screen. Or you may have inadvertently discovered that there are times when Word IA automatically flips you into Web Browse View, such as when you try to access a URL link you've created.

This screen has many other uses, though, not the least of which are browsing the Web straight from your Word interface and copying documents and hyperlinks you find along the way. Because the buttons that replace many of the toolbar items on your screen look so different, you may think you've stumbled into a quiz show at first. Where's the Web? Is it behind Door Number One, Door Number Two or Door Number Three?

Fortunately, there's your familiar File menu up there to remind you that you're still in Word. And if you get lost, you can always find your way home by clicking your heels together and tapping on the pencil icon, which takes you back home to Kansas—the Edit screen. But let's take a look around Oz first and see what adventures there are.

After a tour of the toolbar and menu bar options, we'll get our Internet connection up and set off on a quick trip into the World

Wide Web. There, we'll pay particular attention to explaining how Web pages are composed—useful stuff for designing your own pages. We'll show you how to keep track of the pages you like and would like to come back to with the Favorite Places feature. Finally, we'll have a brief encounter with the other Internet functions—FTP and Gopher—that are possible with Word IA.

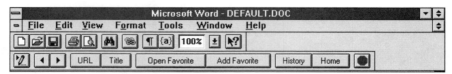

Figure 5-1: *Toolbars in the Web Browse screen.*

File	Edit	View
New...	Can't Undo Ctrl+Z	• Normal
Open...	Can't Repeat Ctrl+Y	Outline
Open URL...	Copy HyperLink	Page Layout
Reload		HTML Edit
Close	Cut Ctrl+X	Full Screen
Close All Documents	Copy Ctrl+C	Load Images [on]
	Paste Ctrl+V	
Save Ctrl+S	Paste Special...	Toolbars...
Save As...	Clear Delete	√ Ruler
	Select All Ctrl+A	
HTML Document Info...		Zoom...
Templates...	Find...	
	Replace... Ctrl+H	
Page Setup...	Go To... Ctrl+G	
Print Preview	Object	
Print... Ctrl+P		
Exit		

Tools	Window	Help
Open Favorite Places	New Window	Internet Assistant for Word Help
Add to Favorite Places	Arrange All	Contents
Macro...	Split	Search for Help on...
Customize...		Index
Options...	Go Back Ctrl+,	
	Go Forward Ctrl+.	Quick Preview
	Home	Examples and Demos
	History List...	Tip of the Day...
	1 DEFAULT.DOC	WordPerfect Help...
	√ 2 NAVIGAT.DOC	Technical Support
		About Microsoft Word...
		About Internet Assistant for Word...

Figure 5-2: *Menus in the Web Browse screen. The menu bar has been artificially stretched to allow all pull-downs to be seen.*

Figure 5-1 is a reminder of the standard toolbars available in this screen, and Figure 5-2 is another of our "stretched" menu bars showing all the pull-down menu options. Practically everything the toolbar does can also be done as a menu choice. The default arrangement is shown here, but of course, as with all Word for Windows screens, you can customize both toolbars and menus. See that Customize option on the Tools menu?

Tour of the Screen

It's worth reiterating that this is *not* the screen you should be using if you want to edit your HTML documents (or someone else's, come to that). In general, this screen is most useful as a tool for verifying links between families of files that you create with the help of Word IA. For checking links to outside Web sites, it functions as an actual Web browser, with your Internet connection up and running. However, you can delay connecting for a short while because there are a few other features to notice first.

Word Standard Options

Even a quick glance at the figures should reassure you that there are plenty of familiar things in what seems at first like a strange land. The File menu's Open, Close and Save functions are all perfectly standard, for a start. Printing—plus its attendant previews and setups—can be done directly from this screen. Toolbar buttons for Find and Show ¶ should ring a bell, as should menu items such as Edit/Go To and Window/Split.

The Edit menu is somewhat strange, to be sure—the Cut, Copy and Paste options are all grayed out, even when there is something on the Clipboard. And although Find and Replace appear to be available, selecting them will simply switch you back to the HTML Edit screen. The fact is that these options are on the Web Browse menus because they are relevant in very special circumstances only.

HTML Options With Local Files

Many options on the Web Browse screen are applicable to your own local HTML documents, and they almost feel like editing. HTML Document Info on the File menu gets you the same dialog box as does the Title toolbar button in the editing screen. The Web Browse screen has a button for this function too, but instead of showing an *i* on a dog-eared page, it boldly says "Title." Pure poetry, to us left-brainers. Note that using the View menu, in addition to zooming in or out, you can place your document in the Full Screen view (Alt+V/U) to see more of its pictures and hyperlinks at once. Using this same menu, you can elect to banish the margins and tabs ruler—a very good idea, since margins and tabs have almost no application on the Web, and you may notice that we drop the ruler from the figures in this chapter. However, if you do banish it, you'll find that it's missing from *all* your Word screens, including desktop publishing documents for which you may need that ruler. Perhaps in the future they'll give us the option of taking the ruler off the Web Browse screen only.

So far as toolbar buttons go, several are useful when dealing with local files. The Back and Forward arrows move you around your family of documents rather smartly. The Forward option is not available until you've executed at least one Back move, since there are normally many possible paths out of a document and the software is not willing to gamble on which one a mere human might mean by "Forward."

The ¶ button functions the same as it does in HTML Edit View to reveal carriage returns and spaces. Likewise, the Html Hidden {a} button brings out the details of your HTML image sources and link destinations. Here's where some normal keyboard edit functions, plus the Edit menu's Cut, Copy and Paste options, come alive again. While you can't edit your text here, you can edit the links. If you're in this window checking your links and you find an error (say, a link to the wrong file), you can display the hidden link coding and correct it without having to switch back to the HTML Edit View.

Browsing the Web

Well, if you're the follow-along type, now's the moment to fire up Trumpet Winsock, Newt or whatever your communication software is and get connected. If you want to see all of the features of this screen, and the different views of a document that you can call up, we need to venture beyond our own desktop or local area network (LAN). Be different if you like, but we're going to the Electronic Frontier Foundation (EFF) because it's a neat page that demonstrates a few things quite well.

When browsing the Web, you can choose whether to download images or not. The Load Images option on the View menu can be toggled on or off (see Figure 5-2). Not loading images will bring you just the text of a page and make things a lot faster; you can always turn images on and reload a page when you want to see its images. Let's leave the Load Images option on for the moment, though, just to make a point.

Hit that big button labeled URL, and up pops a window inviting you to enter an address. The Enter URL box is generously sized—63 characters and scrollable to even more—because URLs can get complicated. However, for now we need just 19 characters:

> http://www.eff.org/

Now press Enter, and we're on the Web and off to Washington, DC, which may be only a step away on the Web, but for us is 2,602 miles by Rand McNally.

Watch closely as EFF's home page comes to you. What happens is that all the text comes down first, then the inline pictures and other hypermedia files one by one. As every picture downloads, a progress bar is superimposed on your screen (see Figure 5-3) giving the name of the file and offering the opportunity to cancel its download. Just as an exercise, let's cancel download of the first image file, EFFlogo.gif, and also click on the big red Stop button at far right on the toolbar. This freezes the page as we have it—text only. If we had been working in Load Images/Off mode, clicking Stop would have been unnecessary—the page would have stopped loading automatically after retrieving the text.

Figure 5-3: *A typical progress bar indicating download of a logo.*

ALT text

Image with
no ALT text

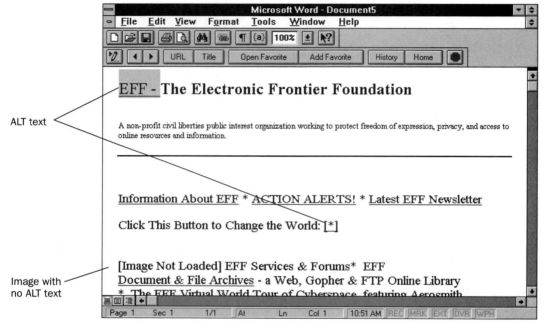

Figure 5-4: *The Electronic Frontier Foundation's home page without any of its inline pictures.*

Analyzing What We See

This is an interesting screen. That EFF at top left is standing in for a pictorial logo, and so is the asterisk following Click This Button to Change the World. The EFF and * are defined as ALT text, exactly as we explained in Chapter 4, "Using Images & Links Creatively." Both of these, plus everything else that's underlined, are hyperlinks. However, the asterisks around ACTION ALERTS, separating the three hyperlinks, are no more than what they seem—asterisks. To the left of EFF Services & Forums you see [Image Not Loaded], which is Word IA's way of telling you that there's a missing image (actually a file-folder icon) for which no ALT text has been specified.

We rate this page as A+ for Web design, for several reasons. Most important, the very first screen gets its primary message across at a glance while giving you plenty of hyperlinks that promise more information on demand. "Click This Button to Change the World" is a cute idea and intriguing, even if it does disappoint by leading to nothing more thrilling than an EFF membership application form. The icons and logos decorating the page are attractive, yet the page does not depend on them for success—it makes perfect sense just as it stands. Finally, when we get to the point of actually loading those images, we will see that they have been kept to reasonably sized files that do not take long to load. So many beautiful Web pages are, to steal a phrase, "born to blush unseen" because it would take the patience of Job to load them completely.

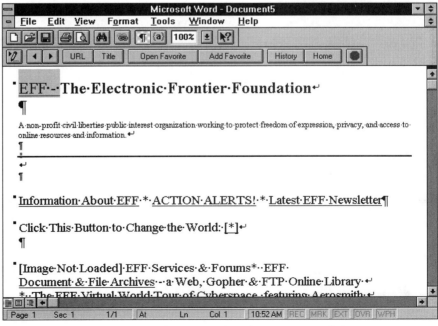

Figure 5-5: *The EFF page with nonprinting characters revealed.*

Alternative Views

We'd like to check the effect of some of the toolbar buttons on this page. Hit that ¶ button and you get something like Figure 5-5. The ¶ symbols themselves basically represent the places where the page author defined paragraph breaks, as you'd expect, and the kinky back-arrows mark places where the author used the HTML tag <BR> to indicate a line break. All other line breaks are "soft" breaks that would change if you picked a different font size.

The ¶ button is a toggle, so we click it again to restore the page to normal, and now hit the {a} button to get this page looking like Figure 5-6.

Inline image

External image: destination of this link

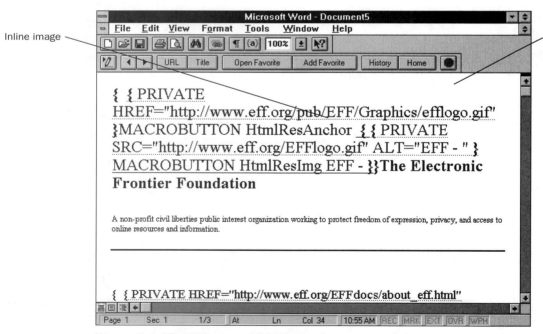

Figure 5-6: *The EFF page with HTML references revealed.*

Now we can see the exact details of the EFF logo hyperlink. The *destination* of the link is the file efflogo.gif in the directory pub/EFF/Graphics/. The *anchor* is a different file, EFFlogo.gif, in the local directory. That's the small (only 1,188 bytes) thumbnail we're expected to click on—but so far all we've seen is the ALT text "EFF," which is a substitute anchor. Typically an external destination file can afford to be way, way bigger and more elaborate. Using a very small thumbnail inline GIF image as a link to a full-screen JPEG image is an extremely common technique.

As you examine these revealed codes, and particularly as you scroll down through the rest of this page and the whole family of pages it leads to, you find out quite a lot about how EFF has structured its directories and organized this Web site. As you might expect from an organization that promotes use of the Internet, EFF is meticulous about its pages. Note how the full URL path to each image is specified, even for tiny little icons. This is not usually necessary—the *relative* path in relation to the current page is usually enough—but using fully qualified URLs is good practice, as long as you have the patience. In Chapter 8, "Tips & Tricks," we'll see how Word IA allows you to specify a *Base URL* for your site, which is a way of guaranteeing that relative links will be sufficient.

Adding the Images

Now it's time to add those missing images and, in the process, learn a few more tricks of the HTML trade. Remember, we're still in Load Images/On mode, but we arrested the download before any images actually arrived. To get the download started again, pick Reload from the File menu (Alt+F/L by keyboard). Reload is a frequently used maneuver on the Web, and many browsers have a big old button especially for it. It reinitiates download of first the text (which should come from cache since we've already grabbed it once), then the pictures—and this time we'll sit back and watch them come down one by one. The result is shown in Figure 5-7.

Inline images used as decoration only

Inline image used as a hyperlink anchor

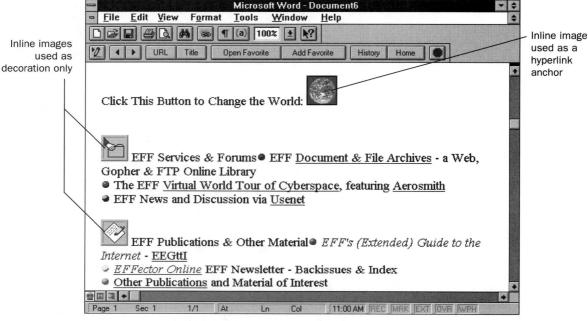

Figure 5-7: *The EFF page with inline pictures added.*

So now we're seeing this page as its author intended, and we notice that only the logo and the world picture are used as hyperlink anchors (meaning that if you click on them, you're taken somewhere else). The other icons and colored balls are used for decoration only. Just to emphasize the point about not making your page design too dependent on images, Figure 5-8 shows this same page as the text browser Lynx sees it. Once again, the designer gets an A+ because the page looks perfectly coherent either way. Now compare Figures 5-4, 5-7 and 5-8, and see how only certain design elements are under control of the author—soft line breaks being one outstanding example of one that is not.

```
                                  Electronic Frontier Foundation  (p1 of 2

              EFF - THE ELECTRONIC FRONTIER FOUNDATION

     A non-profit civil liberties public interest organization working to
     protect freedom of expression, privacy, and access to online resources
     and information.


     INFORMATION ABOUT EFF * ACTION ALERTS! * LATEST EFF NEWSLETTER


     CLICK THIS BUTTON TO CHANGE THE WORLD: [*]



     EFF SERVICES & FORUMS
        * EFF Document & File Archives - a Web, Gopher & FTP Online Library
            * The EFF Virtual World Tour of Cyberspace, featuring Aerosmith
            * EFF News and Discussion via Usenet

     EFF PUBLICATIONS & OTHER MATERIAL
     -- press space for next page --
       Arrow keys: Up and Down to move. Right to follow a link; Left to go back.
     H)elp O)ptions P)rint G)o M)ain screen Q)uit /=search [delete]=history list
```

Figure 5-8: *The EFF page as a text-only Web browser sees it.*

Saving Time

You probably didn't have a stopwatch running as those images
came down, and the time it took would have been dependent on a
host of factors—your modem speed, your geographical location,
the state of the Net today and so on. But we're willing to bet it was
not less than a minute and a half, and that's for a really well-
designed page that keeps its inline illustrations to a minimum.
Getting down the whole of an over-illustrated, pretentious page
can easily give you time for a diet lunch. So now you know why
many people—even users of Netscape, which is much faster than
this—surf the Web in images-off mode, using the ability to scan
the ALT text and elect to bring up only images of special interest.

Keeping Track of Your Web Wanderings

Since we like this page so much, let's make a record of it so that
we can easily come back. Every Web browser has some way of
keeping a list of often-visited Web sites—an extremely valuable
service, since it means you have to enter those long URLs correctly

once only. Admittedly, **http://www.eff.org/** isn't too bad, but one we visit fairly frequently, a repository of interesting clip art to help decorate our pages, is **http://www.cs.yale.edu/HTML/YALE/CS/ HyPlans/loosemore-sandra/clipart.html**. We don't care to type that very often!

Add Favorite

The Netscape Navigator calls these site lists Bookmark lists and Mosaic calls them Hotlists, but here we'll use that big Add Favorite button and, in Word IA terminology, put EFF on our Favorite list. We'll come back for another look at the fave list in a page or two. First, we'd like you to notice that the EFF home page has appeared on another list automatically.

The History List

History

Choose the next button to the right, the one labeled History. (We sure are glad they didn't try to come up with a pictogram for that one!) Up comes something a bit like Figure 5-9, but probably a lot shorter if you've only just begun exploring the Web.

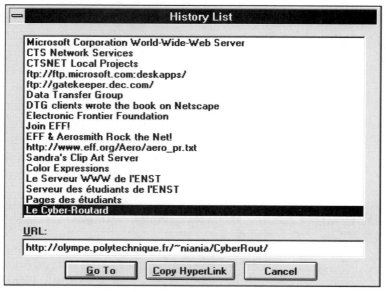

Figure 5-9: *Part of our History List.*

History lists, too, are practically a universal feature of Web browsers, and again Word IA takes a slightly unconventional approach. Netscape and Mosaic don't preserve their history lists when you log off, so the history list is the history of that session only. Word IA, however, writes this list to a file—so this list tends to build up into nothing less than a list of every Web site you've ever visited! (See the sidebar "Managing Your History List" for tips on keeping this under control.)

The History list is highly useful. You can navigate the list using your mouse or your keyboard arrow keys. When you select an item, its URL is displayed in a separate little window and you can hyper off to the page using the Go To button. With the Copy Hyperlink button, you can place a hyperlink to the URL on the Clipboard, ready to be dropped into another document. The software is clever enough not to keep on listing the same site, so if you're the type who feels the urge to check the Tarot page at UCLA 10 times a day, your guilty secret is safe and your History list uncluttered. The only downside is that this is a completely unsorted list, unlike your Favorite list, which can be ordered into a paragon among sorted and categorized lists, as we shall soon see.

Managing Your History List

As we implied in the main text, the size of your History list can matter quite a bit. You may be thinking how great it would be to have a complete record of every Web page you visit but, as they say, be careful what you wish for lest your wish be granted. In a year's time, will you *really* be glad to have an unsorted list of 2,000 sites?

Word IA tries to protect you from your own rashness by limiting the length of this list to 50 by default, but here's how to change this to whatever suits you:

The list is kept in a file called htmlhist.ini in your windows directory. Open that file. It is a pure ASCII text file, and it must stay that way. Therefore, if you have Confirm Conversions checked in the Open dialog box, *make sure you open this file*

as Text Only. **When the file turns up in your edit window, you
will recognize it easily enough. At the top you should see this:**
  MRULength=50
**Simply change the figure 50 to whatever else you have decided
would suit you.** *We do not recommend that you attempt any
other editing of this cross-referenced file.*

The Favorite List

When Word IA is all freshly downloaded, the Favorite list looks
like Figure 5-10, with just one single item.

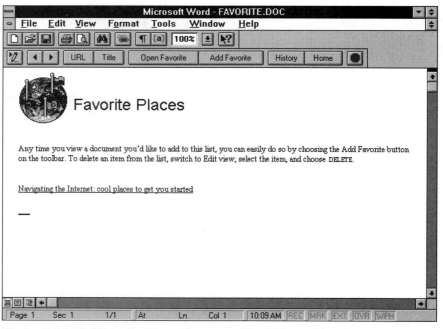

Figure 5-10: *The Favorite Places document Word IA provides to get you
started.*

Click on that item and it sends you off to **http:// www.microsoft.com/pages/deskapps/word/ia/getstart.htm**, and thence off into the wide blue Web yonder. As you wander the Web, from this or any other starting point, you can start adding to that list simply by clicking on the Add Favorite button.

Now, if we told you how to be all disciplined about creating your Favorite list right from the start, you'd just ignore us anyway, so we're not going to bother. Our official advice is to go away and start accumulating hot sites in random fashion, then come wailing back to this chapter saying, "My list is too long and I don't know how to organize it. WAAAAA!!!!! What Now????"

Ready for Some Help Now?

OK, here's your re-entry point to the chapter, with an out-of-control Favorite list that needs discipline. It might look something like this:

Navigating the Internet: cool places to get you started
Data Transfer Group
Washington WebCrawler
CUI W3 Catalog
HotWired: New Thinking for a New Medium
WWWW - the WORLD WIDE WEB WORM
Yahoo
America's Cup On-Line
Shakespeare texts
Le Cyber-Routard
Virtual Frog Dissection Kit Info Page
Mark Rosenstein's Sailing Page
SAN DIEGO ENTERTAINMENT GUIDE
Electronic Cafe
The Exploratorium
The WebMuseum
IRC pictures of the rich and famous, Soton
The Magazine Rack: Sunset
.net - Index
The Internet Movie Database at Cardiff UK
Screenwriters/Playwrights Page
Current Weather Maps/Movies
Page d'accueil de l'ICIST

Kaminski Info-Deli
Gopher jewels
Ventana Online Companion

The first thing you have to realize is that what you are looking at is a file called c:\winword\internet\favorite.doc. It is not, in fact, an HTML file, although it has hyperlinks and behaves exactly as if it were. But there's nothing magic or untouchable about this file. *You can edit it however you like,* changing its order, making indents, lists and fancy boxes, just as if it were a desktop publishing file (which is exactly what it is).

So let's take this list in hand and make it into *our* list instead of a generic one. We'll be conservative and make a safety copy of it as favorite.was, just in case. Now we can get to work. For a start, the list breaks one of the rules of Web page design—its first screen does not concentrate on giving information. That decorative logo may be pretty, but it's taking up too much space—the actual list of sites doesn't start until almost halfway down the screen, leaving space for only eight items. We're going to eighty-six it, along with the two-line instruction that we needed to see only once or twice at the most. We'll delete all that, allow just one main heading instead and presto! We've gained space for five more items already (see Figure 5-11). Actually, we could fit 20 or even 30 items on that one screen if we wanted, by placing several on each line delimited by commas or periods or whatever we like. There may be a better way, though.

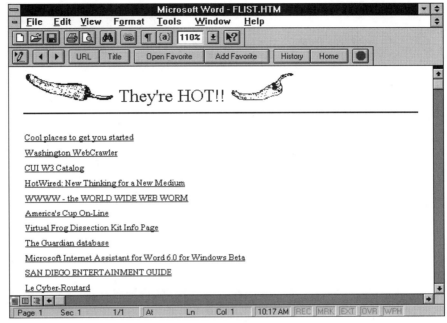

Figure 5-11: *The beginnings of personalization.*

Categorize, Always Categorize

The reason this list is useless is not so much because of its sheer length as the fact that it's unsorted. *HotWired* magazine is sandwiched between two Web searchers, miles away from the two other magazines, and the sailing pages are strewn all over the place. What we're going to do is to enter by hand a bunch of category titles like MAGAZINES, REFERENCE and FUN STUFF. Then we'll simply arrange all of our hyperlinks as indented lists under the appropriate headers. By now you should be used to the idea that when you select a hyperlink anchor phrase and cut it onto the Clipboard, its destination goes along with it.

One little refinement is to end the list with the category title NOT YET SORTED. The reason is that any new sites you add to this list will simply get stuck onto the end. This software may be clever, but it has no way of knowing whether **http:// www.next.com.au/spyfood/geekgirl** is a magazine, fun or even, possibly, sociology. Anyway, here's the list, all straightened out. It took us about 10 minutes.

STARTING POINTS
  Navigating the Internet: cool places to get you started
  Data Transfer Group
  Kaminski Info-Deli
  Gopher jewels
  Yahoo
WEB SEARCHERS
  Washington WebCrawler
  CUI W3 Catalog
  WWWW - the WORLD WIDE WEB WORM
REFERENCE
  The Internet Movie Database at Cardiff UK
  Current Weather Maps/Movies
  Ventana Online Companion
LITERARY
  Shakespeare texts
  Screenwriters/Playwrights Page
EDUCATIONAL
  The Exploratorium
  The WebMuseum
  Virtual Frog Dissection Kit Info Page
SAILING
  America's Cup On-Line
  Mark Rosenstein's Sailing Page
  Page d'accueil de l'ICIST
MAGAZINES
  HotWired: New Thinking for a New Medium
  The Magazine Rack: Sunset
  .net - Index
FUN STUFF
  Le Cyber-Routard
SAN DIEGO ENTERTAINMENT GUIDE
  Electronic Cafe
  IRC pictures of the rich and famous, Soton
OTHER INTERNET RESOURCES
NOT YET SORTED

That listing scheme will probably be adequate for light or medium users of Web resources, with appropriate housekeeping every so often to categorize the NOT YET SORTED list and clear out expired sites (it's amazing—you can find a site that you consider an absolute jewel, then 10 days later you'll be thinking "Why was I interested in a sushi restaurant in Detroit?"). For really heavy users like us, though, sheer length will eventually overwhelm even this type of list. For us, there's an even better way. It's suggested by the way Netscape allows a true hierarchical list; you pull down a list of just your *main categories* first, then click on one to see the list of that category. You can even have second-, third- and fourth-level subcategorization if you really want to get serious about this.

Fragment Your List

To grasp the idea behind the super-list, remind yourself once again that the Favorite list is just a data file, nothing magic, and you can give it exactly the same treatment as you would any other topic you might want to present on the Web in a convenient form. One of the Web design precepts we've been trying to sell you so far is "Make your very first screen tell the story. Let the user decide what details to bring up."

So we're going to follow that principle and fragment the list into nine lists, with a single front page announcing what categories are offered, and all the sublists in separate HTML files hyperlinked to the master list. Once again, we make a safety copy of what we have (this time, favorite.big), just in case we think better of this later on. Now we proceed to dismantle the list section by section. Start by highlighting all of the sites in the starting points category and cut them onto the Clipboard. Now open a new file, attach the Html template to it and paste in all those sites. Save this file as starts.htm. Now bring back favorite.doc (this file name must not change) and turn the header STARTING POINTS into a hyperlink anchor to the file starts.htm.

Switch over to Web Browse View and see what happens when you click on STARTING POINTS. Of course, it brings you a list of all your hot sites in that category to choose from. You could also make a hyperlink return to favorite.doc, but that Back button does the job perfectly well.

So now you just repeat that process for all your categories, and you end up with an ordered family of files and a front page you can take in at a glance.

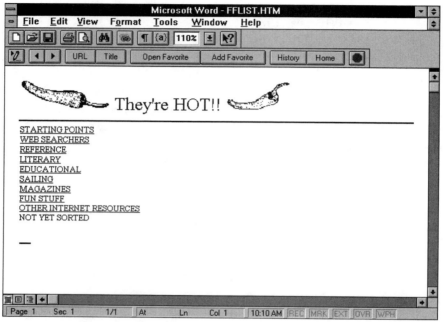

Figure 5-12: *The ultimate hotlist: Click and go.*

The Other Web Browser

So far we've been busy telling you about all the things you can do and places you can go using the Web Browse View. Now it's time to admit it: this Web cruising business is pretty slow when you have to do it with all of Microsoft Word's powerful word processing software competing for your computer memory. Truth is, if you're going to do some serious Web cruising, you're going to need an independent Web browser.

We've already demonstrated that some of the attributes Web browsers can use to display documents do not display the same in Word IA, and in the next chapter we'll discuss a few more. Once you get around to using some of these slightly more complicated codes, you'll want to have another Web browser to check how your page is going to look to your potential Web site visitors.

The fact is, you already have it. You may have picked up a few clues to this buried treasure already in this book. Now we'll show you how to find it. Try this:

1. Open your Internet connection using your communications software.

2. Now fire up Word and immediately switch to Web Browse View.

3. Use the Open URL command and enter an FTP address. Just for illustration, let's use **ftp://gatekeeper.dec.com/pub**.

Now drum your fingers on your desk for a Microsoft minute or two. After a little while you'll see a screen that says, "Click right mousebutton in object to view options." *Don't* click the right mouse button. (The message actually refers to options you'll get *after* you've entered the FTP site—at the moment you'll get only the usual editing options.) Let your machine churn on a little while longer (it may flash a second "Click right mousebutton..." message before settling). Eventually, one of two things will happen: either the FTP screen will appear as an embedded object in your Web Browse screen or, if you're lucky, a screen like that in Figure 5-13 will pop up. What's this!?

That, my friend, is a *real* Web browser. It's called InternetWorks, developed by BookLink Technologies, Inc., which is now wholly owned by America Online. This is a "lite" version of the Web browser that AOL makes available to its customers. The fact that this screen can be made to appear is an artifact of the shotgun marriage between Microsoft Word and InternetWorks that we referred to in Chapter 1, "The Wonderful Web."

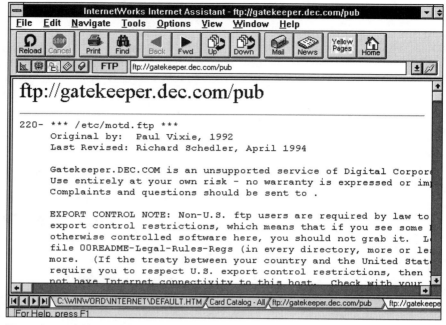

Figure 5-13: *This is a modified version of America Online's Web browser, InternetWorks, which Word IA uses to do FTP.*

We should warn you that the appearance of this InternetWorks screen is a bit erratic, and it may not happen at all on your system, but that doesn't mean that it isn't there behind the scenes doing Word IA's work in FTP. If you did the default installation, you'll find the file iwia.exe in c:\winword\internet. If you want to do some serious Web cruising and have no other dedicated Web browser, you can make this into a program item in Windows and use it on its own, without ever firing up Word. Run the File/New/Program Item option in Windows and enter the file name and path. InternetWorks will kindly provide you with its own icon.

You won't, of course, be able to use any of the editing functions of Word IA when you're in InternetWorks, but you'll find it zips around the Web a lot faster. We can't promise how much longer this will be around (there are obviously development plans in mind, both for Word IA and InternetWorks), but for now, you can use it not only for downloading files through FTP, but for general Web cruising as well.

Since this is *not* a book about InternetWorks, nor about the intricate politics of the software industry, you're on your own in figuring out what everything on the InternetWorks Internet Assistant menu does. *Except,* since they left us no option and we don't want to strand you here in a strange land, we'll tell you how to get in and out of FTP and take some useful loot home.

FTP

For you newbies, FTP (File Transfer Protocol) is just a way of transferring files posted at another computer site to your own computer. There are many, many FTP archives available on the Internet, some of which contain freeware or shareware like Word IA, and some of which contain just general information or fun stuff.

If you have gone to the FTP address we gave you above, **ftp:// gatekeeper.dec/com/pub**, scroll down the page and you'll see the directory of what's available here. (See Figure 5-14.) These are all subdirectories whose names appear alphabetically at the end of each item. Scroll down to the item that says "recipes" and click on it.

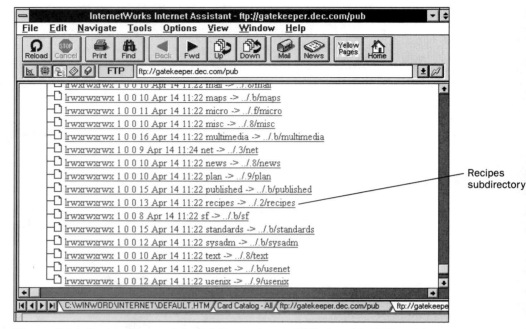

Figure 5-14: *Recipes is one of the subdirectories you'll find at this FTP archive site.*

The recipes subdirectory is a big file that will take some time to reach your desktop, so while you're waiting, we'll tell you a little bit about it. This is an archive of recipes, many of which have appeared in the USENET newsgroup devoted to food topics. All the items are contributed by ordinary Netfolk like you and then selected and edited for posting by a moderator. (You can't access USENET newsgroups with Word IA, by the way—at least not yet—but you may have other ways to access the USENET through your Internet connection. If you're interested, speak to your system administrator.)

Okay, maybe you've got the list by now (and maybe not—it all depends on the speed of your connection, but be patient). What you'll see is a list of recipes. Each one is an actual text document. (See Figure 5-15.) Take your pick and just click on what gets your saliva going. Soon enough you'll have a recipe for apple pie or chicken gumbo right in front of you. Save it to your own disk, and it's yours. That's FTP in a nutshell.

To back out of all this and go back to your Word screen, click on the Back button or simply close InternetWorks. You'll need to close down the message screen that says "Click on the right mousebutton...." Word persists in the delusion that this is an actual document you might want to save.

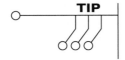

TIP

The recipe files in this archive can be collected into an ongoing Internet cookbook. If you look at one, you'll see formatting codes such as .RH and .IG scattered throughout. These codes are intended to be interpreted by the UNIX typesetting program troff (an explanation is contained in the files intro.doc and recipes.doc in the Programs subdirectory), but they download just fine as Text Only documents. You'll be able to read them on your screen, edit out the troff codes and print them.

Figure 5-15: *We're about to download a recipe for chestnut stuffing from the archives at this FTP site.*

Gopher

Another of the older forms of Internetting, and in many ways the forerunner of the Web, is the Gopher system. The Gopher, developed at the University of Minnesota, aims to link together electronic resources on the Internet by means of a simple menu structure. You choose which topic, or Gopher burrow, you want to explore and get closer and closer to your quarry as you work your way along. At first glance the Gopher may seem like nothing more than an infinite series of menus, with no dinner ever being served. But in actual fact, it's an efficient way of searching for specific topics that interest you without having to bother with a lot of arcane UNIX commands.

Word IA allows you to access Gopher menus through the Web Browse View the same as any URL, except in this case all addresses are prefaced by **gopher://** instead of **http://**. To have a look at what this is all about, go the mother of all Gopher resources, the Gopher Jewels site maintained by the University of Southern California. Open the URL window and patiently and carefully enter this address:

gopher://cwis.usc.edu:70/11/
Other_Gophers_and_Information_Resources/Gopher-Jewels

Add this to your Favorite list right away, so that if you want to come back here you won't have to type that in again!

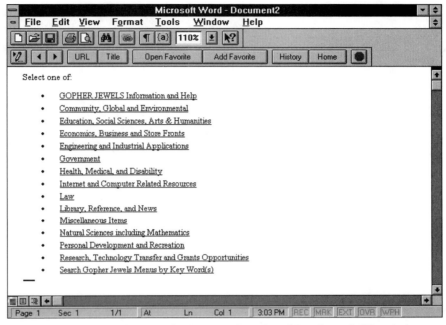

Figure 5-16: *The Gopher Jewels site at University of Southern California is a good starting point for Gopher searches.*

On the first screen you get (see Figure 5-16), you can choose a topic you'd like to search for, go to information about the Gopher or search the Gopher using keywords.

If you choose Government from the list, you can then choose from different government bodies. Choose State Government and see what information is available on the Gopher for your state. For a good illustration of what's in the future, choose Virginia State Government Information, then the Blacksburg Electronic Village.

The Blacksburg Electronic Village (see Figure 5-17) is a project designed to bring together all of the public resources of the city of Blacksburg, Virginia, on the Internet, so that all citizens can have easy access to information about government agencies, hospitals, libraries, parks and recreation, etc. It's one of the most thorough community efforts in electronic linking that exists on the Net right now and a model, perhaps, for many cities in the future. A number of these resources are also available through Web pages— which brings us to another point.

As the Web has begun to prove its superior user-friendliness, many Gopher sites are now being replaced by Web sites. But until indexing services for the Web get up to speed, the Gopher remains a very good way of searching the Net.

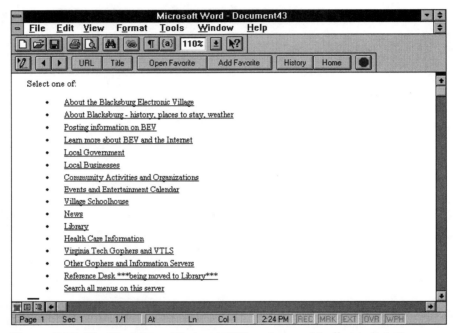

Figure 5-17: *The Blacksburg Electronic Village is a model effort to link the resources of the city of Blacksburg, Virginia, via the Internet.*

Moving On

If you've never seen a Web browser or ventured out on the World Wide Web before, chances are you entered this chapter with a little trepidation. By now you should be feeling a lot more confident as you see the wide, friendly variety of things out there in Web space and how easy it is to become part of it.

As you continue your Web wandering, you may see things you like and want to imitate on your own pages. When you do, remember that you can save any file to your own computer and analyze it later. What looks complicated now will probably become a lot plainer in Chapters 7 and 8 as we look at some of the more specialized things we can do in HTML page design.

In the next chapter, we'll get back to the business of designing our Web pages. We'll show how you can take existing Word documents and turn them into HTML documents, then edit them to make sure they look the way you want them to on the Web. We'll see what works and what doesn't, and how to fix it when it doesn't.

6

Converting Word Documents to HTML

The outstanding advantage of having an HTML editor copackaged with the leading Windows-based word processor is that existing documents—even the lavishly illustrated reports and manuals of the World Wide Widget Corporation—can be converted to Web pages almost instantaneously.

In this chapter, we'll take some existing Word documents, turn them into Web pages and see what works and what doesn't. Certain document elements, such as annotations, borders, column styles and footnotes, have no equivalent on the Web and therefore cannot be used on a Web page. Other elements, such as indented quotes and some embedded artwork, are lost in conversion but are quite easy to reinsert into an HTML file. We'll explain how to take account of these complications and adjust converted documents for better Web presentation.

What Works, What Doesn't

Now that you understand a little bit about HTML, you can understand why some things that work on a Word document might not work on a Web page in HTML. We've already noted that fonts are not under your control in a Web page. Likewise, certain formatting options have no equivalent in HTML.

When possible, Word IA tries to take account of Word formatting features and translate them into an equivalent format in HTML. For example, headings that have been created using the Style list (where heading levels have designated font assignments) will automatically be assigned the appropriate heading level. Headings created simply by choosing fonts, independent of the Style list, will not be preserved.

TIP
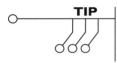

If you get daring and try to insert into an HTML document some elements that you suspect may not be compatible, don't necessarily believe what you see. An example is a Word Art file, which can look as though it has been successfully copied into HTML from the Clipboard. However, it's not really there—if you save, close and reopen your file, you'll find it has evaporated like the dew on a summer morning.

Elements That Don't Convert
Certain elements and formatting options in a Word document will not translate to an HTML document. Word IA does its best to come up with equivalents, but some elements will inevitably be lost or need adjustment after conversion. Among the elements that are not converted to HTML are

- **character formatting (fonts, superscripts, subscripts)**
- **footnotes and endnotes**
- **figure captions**
- **tabs in any paragraph style other than PRE (preformatted text) and DL (definition list)**

- **columns**
- **index and table of contents entries**
- **headers and footers**
- **page breaks and section breaks**
- **annotations and revision marks**
- **borders and shading**
- **frames**
- **drawing layer elements**
- **graphics embedded via the Clipboard**
- **embedded objects, or "cut and paste" objects, such as equations, clip art, Word Art and MS Draw objects**
- **fields (only the field result is converted)**

Some of these elements will have equivalents in HTML 3, which is still developing. Some of the forthcoming HTML 3 conventions are explained in Chapter 8, "Tips & Tricks." For others, there are workaround solutions, some of which are illustrated in this chapter.

Converting Word to HTML

Any document that can be opened in Word can be converted to HTML with Word IA. That includes documents created with WordPerfect or any DOS or Windows-based text editor, and documents in ASCII or Rich Text Format (RTF). Word IA automatically translates Word styles into the closest HTML equivalent.

To convert a document to HTML, you must first open it in Word and then save it as an HTML file type:

1. Choose Open from the File menu (Ctrl+O). Select the file you want to convert and choose OK.

2. From the File menu, choose Save As.

3. In the Save File As Type drop-down box, select HyperText Markup Language (HTML).

4. Change the name of your file, if you wish, and give it the extension .htm. Then choose OK.

If the file you're converting has the .doc extension (Word's default), you need not enter the .htm extension here; Word IA changes it for you. However, if your original file has an extension other than .doc, you must change the extension or the entire file name yourself to avoid overwriting the original.

A Simple Document Conversion

For our first document conversion, we'll take the simple press release in Figure 6-1, created with Word. A quick look tells us there are just one or two things to look out for in the conversion. First, we should check to see if the headings were created using styles. If the headings were created by simply choosing fonts, without reference to a heading style, they're liable to be lost. In this case, we're not sure. So the best thing to do before we convert

---

FACT SHEET

MARCH 1995 - FOR IMMEDIATE RELEASE

What is SEASOIL™

SEASOIL a valuable by-product of the kelp industry, which has been conducted in Southern California for more than 50 years. Kelco harvests kelp from the plentiful beds that lie just offshore, and processes it in a modern plant in San Diego. The primary product, called algin, is used widely in the food, textile and paper industries. The secondary product SEASOIL is a soil amendment, whose high water-retention and other properties make it beneficial for agriculture and landscaping.

Properties of SEASOIL™

As one might expect, SEASOIL is somewhat salty unless specially treated. The air-dried product typically has a salinity in the same range as most manures. It is also highly alkaline, as are most composts and manures. Since high salinity and pH are not favorable characteristics for many agricultural uses, Kelco has developed a process that uses a belt press process to improve the chemistry of SEASOIL. Salinity of the pressed product is reduced to a level suitable for salt-sensitive plants; pressed SEASOIL is also treated to make it more acidic.

Perhaps the outstanding quality of SEASOIL is its very high water-retention, arising both from the algin residues it contains and also from admixture of perlite. This quality makes it ideal for use in areas such as inland California and Baja California that lack sufficient water for many crops that might otherwise enjoy the region's plentiful supply of sunshine, and in the commercial plant-growing industry of San Diego County.

Uses of SEASOIL™

Air-dried SEASOIL has been shown to be beneficial for raising salt-tolerant crops such as oats and barley, even on land that was hitherto barren. An accompanying photograph clearly shows better development of barley in SEASOIL than stalks grown in control soils using standard farming practice.

The pressed product is now well established, both through scientific trials and in industrial test marketing, to have wide application in agriculture, horticulture, landscaping and turf-making (some examples can be seen in accompanying photos). A pilot project conducted in Riverside County in 1994 reported a doubling of fava bean yield, and a tripling of corn yield, when those crops were grown in SEASOIL-amended soils. Another trial, conducted at the University of California at Riverside, showed a dramatic improvement in yield of zucchini, among other crops.

In horticulture, SEASOIL has been shown to stimulate plant growth and development when used as a component of potting soil mixed with standard augmenters such as sand, sawdust or peat. In agricultural use it is normally tilled regularly into the natural topsoil. It is delivered to agricultural sites in bottom-dumping trucks, and dumped out into long furrows. These furrows may remain for many months until the time comes to spread the SEASOIL evenly to a depth of two to four inches and then turn it into the soil with a disc harrow. The site is then ready for planting.

Where has SEASOIL been used?

SEASOIL has been used primarily in the United States for urban landscaping projects. Some ranches in Baja California are now using SEASOIL, notably in the region to the south of Tecate. These ranches have low fertility soil and a great—indeed famous—lack of water, and so the terrain is well suited for SEASOIL's amazing water-retention and nutrient boost. The result has been to turn land with little use into productive farmland, growing crops mainly used as cattle feed at little or no cost to local landowners.

Quantities of SEASOIL shipped across the border have been sufficient to cover about 300 acres to a depth of two inches. The potential beneficial use of SEASOIL in this region is, in fact, much greater—Kelco plans to ship and incorporate SEASOIL into over 1,000 acres of Baja farmland by the end of 1995.

Pressed SEASOIL is now being produced in semi-commercial quantities, and its added value is a part of the overall algin cost-reduction program. We currently have firm orders for a quarter of the product we could produce. By 1996 we anticipate being able to market 100% of the pressed SEASOIL produced, thus significantly reducing costs.

ACCOMPANYING PHOTOS:

1] Barley stalks grown in two inches of SEASOIL, compared with two controls.

2] Impatiens grown in 40% SEASOIL, 60% Metromix.

3] Site of the SEASOIL field study at Rancho Bateques. The study was carried out by the Autonomous University of Baja California.

Figure 6-1: A press release we want to convert to HTML.

it is to use the Autoformat option on the Format menu. That way, Word will attempt to identify anything that appears to be a head with a heading style.

Other elements at a glance on this page that we suspect may not convert are the drawing box with the date at the top and the trademark symbol. But let's convert the page and see.

1. After autoformatting, choose the Save As option from the File menu.

2. In the Save File as Type box, change the file type to HyperText Markup Language (HTML). Since this document has the .doc extension, the extension will automatically change to .htm.

3. Now choose OK. Voilà! Figure 6-2 shows the result.

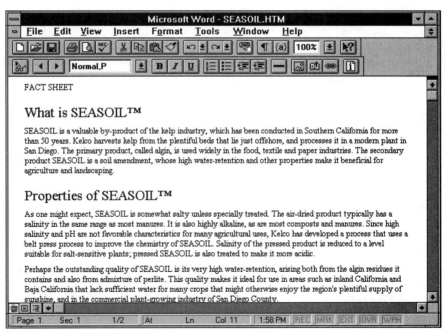

Figure 6-2: *This press release loses very little in conversion to HTML.*

As expected, we lost the drawing box with the date in it—but it's an easy matter to put the date back in. If you really hate to type (or if you come across text boxes containing whole paragraphs), you can copy it to the Windows Clipboard from the original document and drop it in. Unexpectedly, our main header, "Fact Sheet," did not get translated as a level-one head, but we can quickly apply the right heading style using the Style list. Also, it seems the trademark symbol did translate, despite our misgivings. In fact, this is one of the special symbols, or "entities," that HTML allows for (see Appendix C).

Now that it's an HTML document, we can fancy it up with rules and pictures if we like. And don't forget to add the address information at the bottom before posting it. But it's practically ready to go. Altogether not a bad job.

Converting a Brochure

Now let's go one step further in complication. We have some copy of a similar nature we've prepared for the World Wide Widget Corporation, but we've done it up in a brochure style for general distribution about our company. You can see our trifold brochure in Figure 6-3. This could be a good start for the "Our Company" information we teased on the Widget home page.

There's a lot more stuff to be suspicious about here—graphical elements and pictures and special text alignments that we're not sure how Word IA will handle. We know right away that HTML can't display the columns. Even if it could, it wouldn't be appropriate in this case because the brochure is designed to work as a trifold (and nobody's figured out yet how to trifold a computer screen). We *could* take the brochure copy, remove the column formatting and change the page orientation before converting it. But let's just see what Word IA does with it if we don't bother.

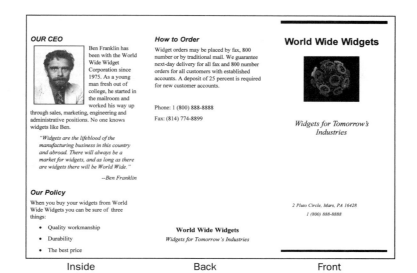

Inside   Back   Front

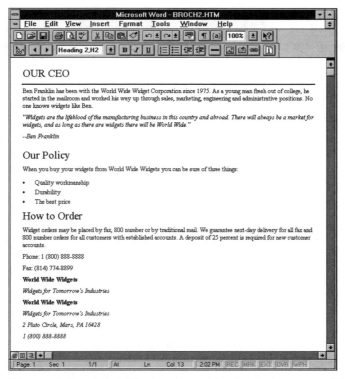

Figures 6-3 and 6-4: *The brochure at top has lost some graphic elements in the conversion, but they can easily be replaced.*

Figure 6-4 shows the result of our conversion. We've artificially extended the screen so you can see how Word IA has treated all the information on the first page, which formed the outside of our brochure. Of course, it had no way of knowing the columns were not in sequential order, so it has simply presented the inside, back and front cover text in that order, as laid out on the page, discarding our column format.

The graphics were not preserved at all, although Word IA has interpreted our drawing box around the CEO's picture as a rule. We can put his picture back in now by using the Picture button and selecting the .gif we've made of it with a scanner. Our CEO's quote is no longer indented, though the italics were preserved. We can turn that into an indented Blockquote in a trice using that option on the Style list.

Our bulleted list was correctly interpreted and preserved, as were all our paragraphs and heads, with the exception of the special type we used on the front cover and the bottom of the back cover. Word IA has given them to us as straight text so we can re-spec them as we wish. The logical thing would be to take the front cover type for "World Wide Widgets" to the top of the file and give it a heading style, then apply the Address style to the rest of the address and phone information (deleting the second occurrence).

We can reorder the information here and add in our pictures and rules as we please, but as you can see, we've got a pretty good start for a Web page about our company. In the end, this was probably easier than reordering our original file, since the special formats and drawing objects would have gotten in our way.

Converting a Newsletter

Now let's really put Word IA to the test. Let's give it something really complicated to convert. Figure 6-5 shows a newsletter we created for the World Wide Widget Corporation. Right away we can see there are several elements on this page that won't translate to HTML.

Figure 6-5: *The newsletter we wish to convert to HTML.*

Figure 6-6 shows what happens to the newsletter file when we convert it to HTML. Not too bad, really. As expected, our graphical elements are gone, as are the columns. But the good news is that the text of our boxed table of contents at the bottom of the page has been preserved. We can see the beginning of some nice hyperlinks out of that.

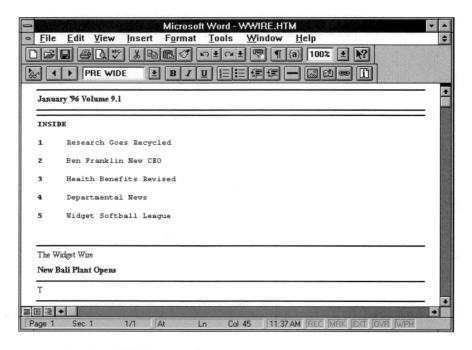

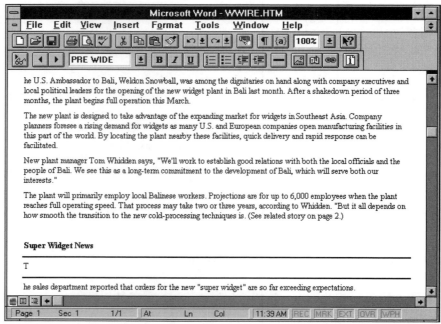

Figure 6-6: *Two screens from the converted document; several elements are misplaced, but the main text looks okay.*

Word IA's conversion program didn't quite know what to do with our raised capital letters, so it's given them to us in ordinary text with rules around them—kind of silly, but easy to fix. The heads for our articles did not translate into HTML heading styles, probably because they had fonts chosen for them outside of the Style list. Another easy thing to fix.

We could just fix those things and call it done, if we wanted to be quick about it. But there's a lot of potential here that we'd like to explore.

First, let's take our newsletter title, which has ended up a little further down than it belongs, move it up and give it an H1 designation. We'll give our articles H2 level heads, then get rid of the extra rules and the initial letters that did not translate to HTML and replace them in the text.

Then there's that table of contents. The two articles on our front page don't have entries because, as originally designed, this included only the inside contents. So we'll want to add those. In trying to do so, we quickly discover that the table of contents is not a real list at all—that is, it's not formatted as a list in HTML. In converting our box, Word IA figured the most reliable way to handle it was to give it the PRE designation. In fact, it's given it a PRE WIDE designation, to take account of the extra space these occupied in the box on our front page.

The <PRE> tag is used by HTML to present text exactly as typed, without any HTML style formatting. It is often used in presenting items like tables. PRE text is usually displayed in a fixed-width typewriter, or monospaced, font.

Preformatted Text

Standard preformatted text assumes a line width of 80 characters and normally wraps at that width. Word IA renders this by default as nine-point Courier on an eight-inch ruler.

In HTML, the <PRE> tag may be modified to specify a line width, although not all browser software respects the WIDTH= modifier. Word IA offers the style option PRE WIDE, which specifies 132 characters and is rendered in eight-point Courier on a 14-inch ruler. Lines in this style are liable to bleed off users' screens, but of course horizontal scroll bars are a feature of all Windows-based browsers.

To see the HTML formatting that's been assigned, move your cursor down the left edge of the screen using your keyboard arrow keys and watch the Style list box change for each new format code it comes across. (See Figure 6-7.)

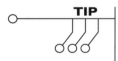

TIP

After the rules and at the top and bottom of the PRE list you'll notice a little code called Restart List in the Style list box. This is not really an HTML code at all. It's used by Word IA to separate certain elements like horizontal rules and lists. For all practical purposes, you can ignore it. Do not attempt to use it in your authoring, as it is not preserved in HTML.

HTML declares our text to be preformatted, at 132 characters per line.

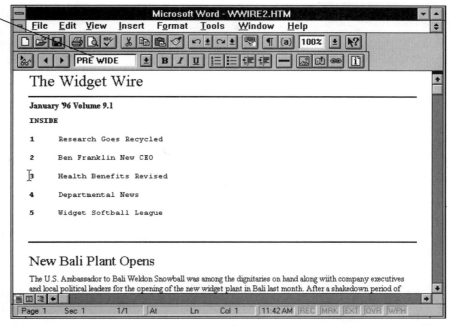

Figure 6-7: *The Style box shows that the text of our table of contents is actually not a list, but preformatted text.*

To convert this PRE text into a real list in HTML—and in the process get rid of the rather unappealing typewriter script that many Web browsers display PRE text in—we need to get rid of the PRE formatting designation. This will take several steps because not only is this not a real list, but Word IA has also inserted a code for line breaks (<BR>) at the end of each item. If we tried to turn this into a list right away by blocking the items and applying the numbered or bulleted list style, Word IA would treat the entire list as one list item containing several lines, since there are no paragraph breaks.

Take the following steps to convert this table of contents into a proper list:

1. Use the arrow keys to move your cursor down the left edge of the screen, starting at the top of the PRE section. Delete the number and extra spaces at the beginning of each list item.

2. Place the cursor at the beginning of each item, starting with the first, and use the Backspace key to delete the line breaks and any extraneous spaces. Then press Enter to insert a new line break at the end of each item. (Don't forget to do the same to the last item.)

3. Block the entire PRE text and then apply the Normal,P style using the Style drop-down list. Add any other items you want to include in the list.

4. Block all the list items and apply the numbered or bulleted list style using the List button, the Style drop-down list or the Format menu commands.

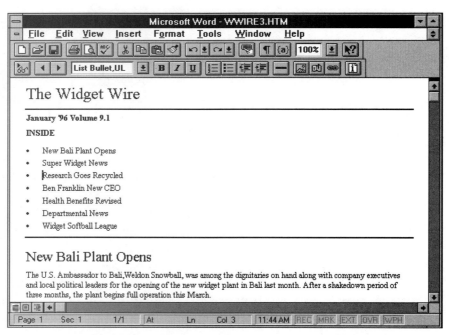

Figure 6-8: *We've fixed our list now, and we're ready to put in hyperlinks and add some decoration.*

Now we're ready to turn our list items into hyperlinks. We'll first go down and place a bookmark at the beginning of each article. Then we'll return to our list and make hyperlinks to our bookmarks. (See "Bookmark Button" and "Hyperlink Button" in Chapter 3.) If this were a very big document, we might consider breaking it up and making separate files for each of our articles.

Finally, we're ready to add a little decoration. We'll replace a couple of the horizontal rules around the table of contents with colored bars as GIF files. Then we'll resize and insert the pictures we used to illustrate a couple of our articles. (See "Picture Button" in Chapter 3 and "Advanced Image Options" in Chapter 4.)

Now, about those drop caps (the big decorative letters starting a paragraph): Most people would let them go because they aren't used in HTML. But we've become perfectionists now. We restore a drop cap by using not a letter, but a *picture* of a letter. Using CorelDRAW! (or any of a number of other graphics applications), we simply make up a 72-point capital *T* with a border around it, and save it as tee.gif. Now it can be sized to about 50 pixels in width and inserted just like any other GIF file. (Don't forget to delete the letter it replaces.) This is a good moment to remind you once again, though, that your readers choose their own font size for the main text, so the overall effect will not be the same for everyone.

Just one more little tweak, and we're done. When we have our fancy *T* in place, we use the Html Hidden {a} button to reveal hidden HTML coding. Where the hidden source code says ALIGN= BOTTOM, we slip a cursor in and edit it to say ALIGN=LEFT instead. This is a bit of a cheat, since the left align is not an officially recognized attribute yet. (See Chapter 8, "Tips & Tricks," for this and other extended codes.) However, Netscape is one Web browser that does recognize it and will display it as text wrapped to the picture, as shown in our final article presentation in Figure 6-10. There's nothing to lose because Word IA is going to show text alignment as BOTTOM no matter what we do.

There! Not bad, if we do say so ourselves.

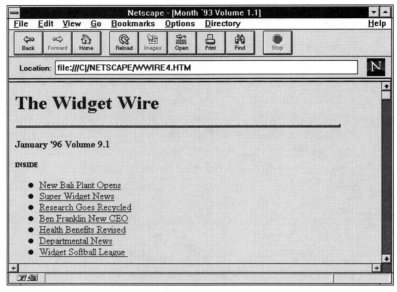

Figure 6-9: *Netscape displays our finished Web page with hyperlinks to the articles.*

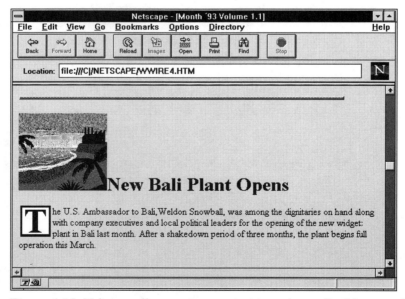

Figure 6-10: *Netscape allows us to wrap text to an image (in this case, a large initial letter in GIF form) by using the ALIGN=LEFT attribute.*

Coping With Tables & Databases

Since HTML was invented originally to serve the internal needs of a scientific laboratory (the European Laboratory for Particle Physics in Switzerland), you might think it would be an ace at things like tabulations and equations. Actually, such exotica have been HTML's weakness so far in its brief history, although the powers that be are now very close to agreeing on conventions for displaying them. (See Chapter 8, "Tips & Tricks," for more on this.)

Until these conventions become accepted and can be interpreted correctly by the popular Web browsers (and they may be adopted by Microsoft for a future update of Word IA), the fallback technique when faced with typographical challenges like this

$$k=\sum 4pn^2\partial y/\partial x(q-\sqrt{n})$$

is to go through a process that amounts to taking a picture of it and inserting it into the Web page as an inline GIF.

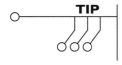

TIP

If equations are your passion, and you know (or think you can learn) the LaTeX format, a conversion package exists that automatically converts LaTeX equations into GIFs. It's called Latex2html, it was invented at the University of Leeds in England and it's available by FTP from this address:
ftp.tex.ac.uk/pub/archive/support/latex2html

Tabulations are in the same position as equations—waiting for acceptance of proposed standards. Meanwhile, they are somewhat easier to cope with, although they can create drudgery for HTML authors. In this case, one technique for fairly simple tabulations is to simply set them out the way you want them, then declare to HTML, "This is how I want it. Hands off." You do this by declaring that section of your document "preformatted"—that is, by applying the Preformatted,PRE style to it. In the previous section, we showed how Word IA used this style to take care of a special formatting problem it had in converting our newsletter.

A Simple Table

Suppose you want to render the following simple table in your home page:

	1991	1992	1993	1994
Sales	12,976.50	14,077.00	13,336.75	20,713.00
Inventory	1,303.00	988.00	714.00	2,021.75
Royalties	8,225.56	5,538.21	10,766.89	4,261.76
Total	*22,505.06*	*20,603.21*	*24,817.64*	*26,996.51*

We laid that out using decimal tabs for alignment and drawing objects for the rules, and it's a fine example of how *not* to do the job, since none of that careful formatting survives translation to HTML, even if you do declare it preformatted. Since tabs and drawing objects are not converted, that table will come out looking like this:

```
1991 1992 1993 1994
Sales 12,976.50 14,077.00 13,336.75 20,713.00
Inventory 1,303.00 988.00 714.00 2,021.75
Royalties 8,225.56 5,538.21 10,766.89 4,261.76
Total 22,505.06 20,603.21 24,817.64 26,996.51
```

If you were working directly in HTML source code, you'd have to start the whole section with the <PRE> tag, then enter your columns of figures using the space bar to align them. Tabs are highly unreliable in HTML since you never know how many spaces a Web browser will expand them to. And those horizontal lines would be a problem because the <HR> tag is not valid within a preformatted section. The *Total* line could still be rendered as italic, using the <EM>. . .</EM> tags, since almost all of the so-called highlighting elements are allowed. Finally, you'd end with </PRE> to signal the end of the section. You can replicate that process, if you wish, by setting up your table in the HTML Edit screen, using the PRE style and spacing it by hand. It will work out fine—but we're about to suggest a better way.

Using the Tools Provided

Now here's the same table created with Word 6.0's table management options, using decimal tabs for the arithmetical cells and the Grid3 style that is one of the options you get when you go for Table/Autoformat:

	1991	1992	1993	1994
Sales	12,976.50	14,077.00	13,336.75	20,713.00
Inventory	1,303.00	988.00	714.00	2,021.75
Royalties	8,225.56	5,538.21	10,766.89	4,261.76
Total	**22,506.06**	**20,603.21**	**24,817.64**	**26,996.51**

Not only do we get a much neater-looking table, but we made use of the built-in formula feature to add the totals automatically (noting with relief that we hadn't made any mistakes in our handmade example). Now Word IA has this information in a form it can understand. The translation to HTML looks like this:

	1991	1992	1993	1994
Sales	12,976.50	14,077.00	13,336.75	20,713.00
Inventory	1,303.00	988.00	714.00	2,021.75
Royalties	8,225.56	5,538.21	10,766.89	4,261.76
Total	22,505.06	20,603.21	24,817.64	26,996.51

A little fix-up is obviously needed to get those decimals aligned, but at least it *looks* like a table. So the straight story on tables is this:

- *Don't* go it alone with tabs and graphics.

- *Do* do it the way Word IA expects you to do it, and the software will help you along as well as it can.

- *Do* expect to do some last-minute tweaking before your Web page looks really satisfying.

In Chapter 8, "Tips & Tricks," we'll show-and-tell a really super table format that isn't yet officially available, but that you can use already.

Database Info

Now take a look at Figure 6-11. This is a section of the World Wide Widget Corporation's latest catalog, which includes part of the database widcost.dat imported as a table, using the same Grid3 autoformat option. There are other elements in the catalog that we're going to be interested in shortly, but for now, just watch what happens when we convert this for use on the Web.

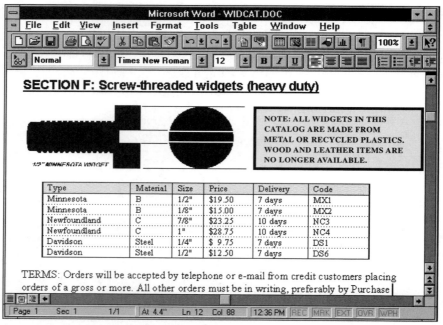

Figure 6-11: *Vital information about the cost of widgets.*

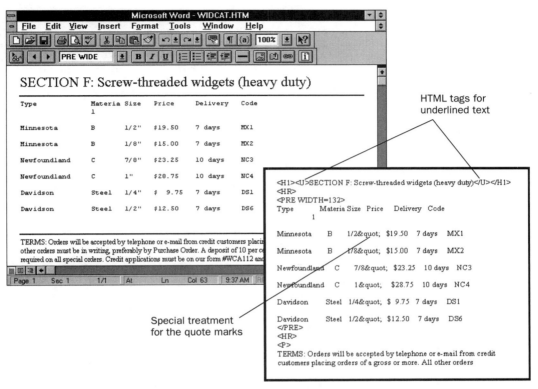

Figure 6-12: *First attempt to convert the catalog to HTML.*

Figure 6-12 shows how Word IA makes the page look; the inset shows the HTML source code that is generated. The <U>. . .</U> tags enclosing the main heading are a faithful way of indicating that this should be underlined, although neither Word IA nor Netscape actually displays underlining (InternetWorks and Mosaic do, however). The <HR> (horizontal rule) tag has been used legitimately here, because both the rules are outside the preformatted section. With a bit more fuss, both this and our previous handmade example could be better presented—the column headings could be within <PRE>. . .</PRE> tags, then a <HR> could create a ruler, then back into <PRE>, and so on.

The $9.75 price went out of alignment, since we're not dealing with decimal tabs here and a space does not have the same width in preformatted HTML as it does in a table. But that's easy to fix by just adding and deleting spaces. Notice, though, the very ugly way Word IA has decided to wrap the column header "Material," with just the *l* arriving on the next line. It was fooled by the very short entries in this column into allocating only seven characters as the column width. Since the spacing between columns really is spacing, not just tab characters, fixing that up is going to be an annoyance. Notice, too, from the inset source code, that Word IA has chosen to make the line width 132 characters, which accounts for the small type.

What Is Wrong With This Picture?

Obviously, one important element of the catalog that did not appear in the HTML version is the illustration. On the one hand, this should not surprise us since embedded images are on the official No Can Do list. On the other hand, though, perhaps it *is* surprising in this case because the picture is in GIF format, and inline GIFs, as we discovered back in Chapter 4, are so common in Web page design that a Web page without one looks as unfinished as an envelope without a postage stamp.

The good news is that it's incredibly easy to put the picture back in. Simply open up a line by adding a hard return after the title, and reinsert the picture using the Image button. The result is shown in Figure 6-13—and for good measure, we've fixed up the table along the lines we just suggested.

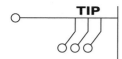

TIP

When we did this, we got a surprise because we'd forgotten we had resized the GIF on the original catalog page, and it came up huge. We had to reduce the picture itself, using our favorite image tweaker, the freeware application LView.

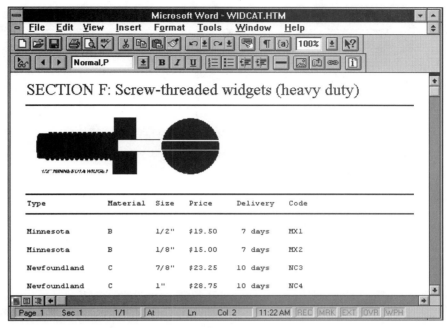

Figure 6-13: *The illustration restored.*

Illustrations for catalogs, brochures and the like that are not in GIF format (actually, bitmapped .xbm images are OK, too) need the extra step of conversion. The recommended way is to cut and paste the image into a graphics application such as Microsoft Imager, CorelDRAW! or Adobe Photoshop, save it in GIF format, then return to your HTML file in Word IA and insert it as before. You may have to hunt around to find an application capable of converting your clip art, and in some cases it may be less trouble to get out there on the Net and browse the oceans of good art in GIF format.

Embedded Objects

That leaves one element of the catalog still missing from its Web page equivalent—the warning box to the right of the illustration (Figure 6-11). This is what's known as an *embedded object*—it's a text box created with the Drawing toolbar, just like the simple box enclosing the date of the press release in Figure 6-1. For the press release, we just retyped the date, but this is enough text that it's worth selecting the text within the box using your mouse, then cutting and pasting to the appropriate place in the HTML document. Very easy.

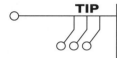
TIP

Embedded objects such as geometric figures, frames, callout leaders and free-form sketches are going to disappear completely when you convert your document to HTML. Remember this, though: when confronted with document elements that don't convert to your satisfaction, you always have one last card up your sleeve. You can print the document, put it in a scanner and turn the element into a GIF file. That way you get exactly the same look on your Web page. When you browse the Web, come across a neato page and wonder, "How did they do that?" that will often be the answer.

Figure 6-14 shows the final look of our widget catalog Web page. Once again, something that looked pretty complicated turned out to be not so hard using Word IA.

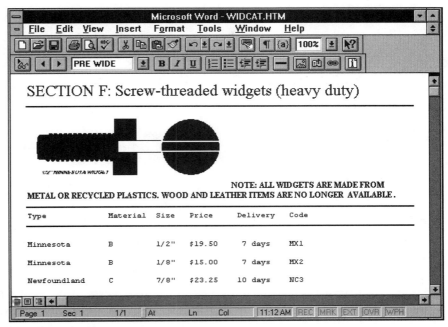

Figure 6-14: *The finished Web page.*

To wrap up, here's some final advice about making tables and special layouts in HTML:

◈ Use the tools available for tables in Word, and Word IA will convert them more reliably.

◈ Use <PRE> if you don't want your text to be formatted with HTML styles, but to be presented exactly as typed.

◈ Remember to use spaces instead of tabs.

◈ Don't use drawing objects like lines and boxes—or if you do, realize they won't be preserved when converted to HTML.

◈ Remember that if you want things just so and all else fails, you can scan a layout or piece of text and make a graphic of it.

If you're really keen on tables, keep abreast of HTML 3 developments. Table specifications are in the works, and you can already implement some of the table tags and have them display on certain browsers by inserting them into a text file. This is one of many examples of Netscape jumping the gun—see Chapter 8, "Tips & Tricks," for more on this.

Moving On

In this chapter, you've seen how Word IA makes it easy for you to convert existing documents into HTML. As you become more familiar with what you can do on a Web page, you'll find better ways to dress up your pages and enhance them for Web presentation.

In the next chapter, we'll talk about some more specialized options available in HTML, including creating forms for user feedback, making sensitive maps and inserting audio and video files. Although all of these may seem intimidating at first, you'll be surprised at how easy they can be.

7

Advanced HTML Options

So you've got this Web page creation business down now, and you're feeling a little bored. Ready for some Web excitement? It's time to talk real Web wizardry. How about creating a response form for your Web visitors? Or some of those great graphics (called *sensitive maps*) that allow users to go to new links by clicking on different parts of the picture? You can create both of these things much more easily than you might think.

And with the right tools, you can add some exciting dimensions to your Web pages. It doesn't take much at all to add sound to your Web page with a link to an audio file, and with a little ambition and some professional tools you can even add video clips.

In this chapter, we'll cover all these things, beginning with forms. Then we'll talk about sensitive maps—a bit of Web magic that's surprisingly easy with the right tools. Finally, we'll delve into the dimensions of hypermedia and tell you how to add sound and video files to your Web pages.

Creating Feedback Forms

The fill-out-and-return type of form is an advanced HTML feature that's well worth learning because it puts you in direct contact with the users of your page. At the simplest level, a form can be used to create a "guest book" so you know who has visited your page. Forms, however, can get very much more complicated than that, and although form fields are available to authors of standard Word 6.0 documents, converting them presents some challenges.

A *form field*, for those of you who are already confused, is simply one of the fields of a fill-in-the-blanks form for responses from users. Word 6.0 allows you to create dynamic form documents that can be filled out onscreen. When finished, these documents function in *protected* mode, meaning that a user can enter text only in certain defined fields. Forms like these are most effective in a local area network (LAN) environment, but their sophistication makes them useful in stand-alone installations as well.

Form fields come in three basic flavors:

❧ *Text form field*—Simply a text box into which the user types a response.

❧ *Check box form field*—A "binary" box that has only two states, checked (yes) and unchecked (no). The user toggles between the two states with the mouse pointer.

❧ *Drop-down form field*—A form field that has a limited number of predefined possible entries, with the list appearing as a drop-down when the user clicks on the field. The time sheet wizard, Weektime, includes an example of a drop-down list in the Status field, where the possibilities are Full Time, Part Time, Temporary, Contractor.

Practically all of Word's form wizards illustrate how you can arrange for explanatory notes to appear in the status bar whenever the user enters a form field.

Figure 7-1 shows a fanciful example that may be a bit more fun than a time sheet. It includes two straight text form fields (Name and Specify other), a check box and two multiple-choice drop-down fields. We've slightly faked this figure to show both drop-down lists exposed in the same frame—in reality, only one could be active at any moment. An important point to grasp is that the curt instruction in the status bar (Donation expected) belongs to the contribution pull-down list and would be seen only when the user is actually making the awesome choice between zero and $50 for Charlie's going-away gift. In Word terminology, it's the *help text* associated with that form field.

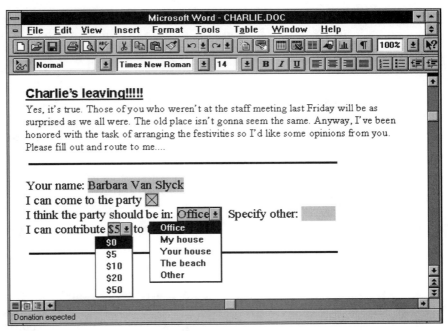

Figure 7-1: *Three types of form field in a simple Word interoffice document.*

Forms Options

Figure 7-2 shows the Word 6.0 Forms toolbar, which you can pop into the foreground of your document as you build a non-HTML form. The three buttons grouped at upper left let you insert fields of the three main types. (Another way is to use the menu option Insert/Form Field and select from three radio buttons.)

The Form Field Options toolbar button brings up a fairly complex dialog box that allows such things as restricting the width and/or format of a field, specifying default field content and triggering macros. It's also here that you enter the help text (if any) that you want to associate with the field you are building.

The Protect Form button is extremely important because the form cannot be used as intended until it's protected from user changes—the drop-downs won't drop, the check boxes won't check and so on. During building of a form, the toolbar Protect Form button is a quick-and-dirty toggle to switch between (1) a mode in which you have complete freedom of editing and (2) a mode in which you see your form as users will see it, and verify that it works as you intend. Once you are satisfied with the form, it's expected that you will protect it more rigorously using the Protect Document option on the Tools menu. That way, you can assign a protection password so that users can't unprotect the form themselves and make unwanted edits such as "Gift for Charlie? *Moi?* Surely you jest."

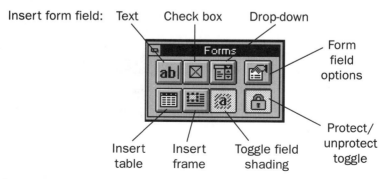

Figure 7-2: *The Word 6.0 Forms toolbar.*

Forms in HTML

What happens if we try to transform the sign-up sheet for Charlie's leaving party into an HTML document, intending to post it on a (presumably local) web? Actually, this particular form is simple enough and compact enough that it translates reasonably well. Not all form designs will fare so well. More importantly, the options available to form builders in the HTML environment are rather different, and if you make your forms in Word and then transform them, you'll be depriving yourself of certain options that you might find very useful, and of one that is absolutely essential. That's why we firmly recommend that—unless you have no choice—you create HTML forms only within HTML documents.

Take a look at Figure 7-3, compare it with Figure 7-2, and see how things change on the Forms toolbar when you're in HTML Edit View. To understand these changes, we have to start at the end, as it were, and get a feel for what happens when somebody enters data into a form on the Web. It has to do with that big Submit button, and it's not like just entering your preferences for Charlie's party and routing the file back to the party organizer.

So what *does* happen to a completed form?

Insert form field: Text   Check box   Drop-down

Form field options   Toggle field shading   Protect/ unprotect toggle

Figure 7-3: *Internet Assistant's Forms toolbar.*

Let's revert for a minute to a boilerplate—the standard name-rank-and-number type of form shown in Figure 7-4—to understand the principle of the thing. Although you don't see them onscreen, each of the fields on this form has been assigned a name by the form's creator. The Name field has been called (inventively) name, Address Line 1 is addr1 and so on. The US Citizen check box is called cit, and the Favorite food drop-down is called gastro. These names are hidden in the source code.

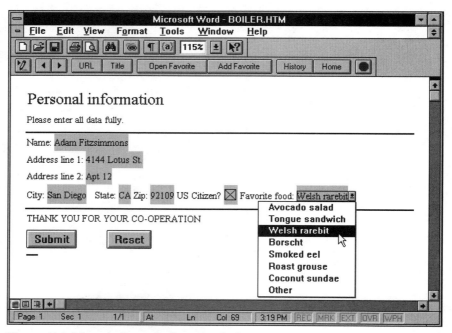

Figure 7-4: *Name/value pairs in a simple form.*

Now, when Adam Fitzsimmons has his form all filled out, he clicks on that Submit button. His personal info is passed to the server computer in a series of what are called *name/value* pairs. Each of these pairs represents the *value* Adam assigned to the field of a given *name*. The whole string that would be passed to the server by this form is

```
?name=Adam+Fitzsimmons&addr1=4144+Lotus+St.&addr2=
Apt+12&city=San+Diego&state=CA&zip=92109&cit=
on&gastro=Welsh+rarebit
```

Never mind for the moment *how* this string gets to the server, or what happens next to pass it to whoever needs it.

Now we know enough to construct our own HTML form, and you won't be surprised to hear that Word IA does its best to make things easy for you.

Building a Form, Step by Step

Continuing the gastronomic theme we introduced in the boilerplate form, we'll now design an online questionnaire for a worldwide restaurant database. The idea is to publish this on the Web and allow all our users to contribute their favorite eating places so that, over time, we will build up an interesting variety of recommendations (we know of at least one such enterprise that's already running on the Web). Here we go, then.

Creating a Text Form Field

The most common form field is the text form field. This is simply a field wide enough for users to type in some information, such as a name or address. Beginning with creating the file for our form, this is the procedure:

1. Open a new file using the Html template. Give it an HTML title (the *i* button) and a file name (Save As).

2. Enter some heading information that will be helpful to users of your form, followed by a horizontal rule.

3. Enter the introduction to your first form field—in our example, it's "Restaurant name:".

4. Now it's time to build your first text field. *Do not use the Forms toolbar for this.* It would work fine for a Word form, but it does not create an HTML form correctly because it does not insert the necessary HTML tags for top and bottom of form. Instead, select the menu item Insert/Form Field (Alt+I/M by keyboard). You will get the information box shown in Figure 7-5. Select Continue.

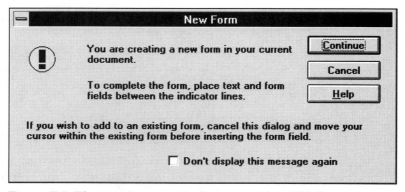

Figure 7-5: *The warning you get when you create a Web form.*

5. Select or accept the Text radio button in the small dialog box that appears (see Figure 7-6), and then select Options. Now the Text Form Field Options dialog box shown in Figure 7-7 appears.

6. Of the array of options this dialog box offers, we're initially interested in just two. First, it's never wise to allow any HTML form field to have unlimited length, so use the tiny up arrow beside the Maximum Length text box to roll from Unlimited up to the appropriate number of characters. For our example, we'll use 30, which simply means that we're restricting the length of restaurant names to 30 characters.

7. Now, in the Field Settings box, look at the label in the Bookmark text box. This is the label that will translate to that all-important Name attribute that will identify the data when a user eventually submits the completed form. Word IA defaults it to Text1 (and so on sequentially after that), but it's good practice to make it more meaningful so you can easily interpret the responses you receive. (We changed ours to rname.) Hit that OK button.

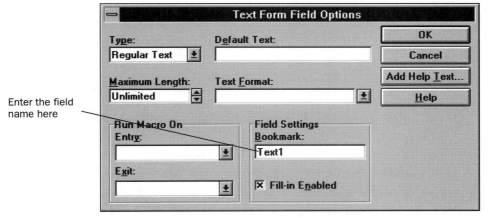

Figure 7-6: *First step in creating a form.*

Enter the field name here

Figure 7-7: *The Text Form Field Options dialog box.*

Your screen should look like Figure 7-8, and now you can immediately understand an important difference between an HTML form and a Word form. In HTML, only a certain specific area of a document (actually, it could be several specific areas) is defined as a form. That section or sections is enclosed between the HTML tags <FORM>...</FORM>, and the form delineators you are now seeing represent those tags unmistakably.

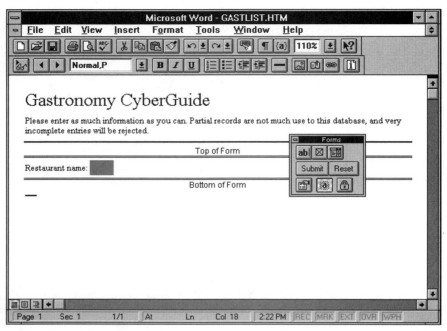

Figure 7-8: *The form area of this document is now clearly defined.*

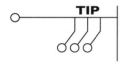

> *To keep the example form in this chapter as clear as possible, we're going to stick to minimal text and decoration and concentrate on the form field options. But the fact that you're working between those form delimiters should not deter you from using a full range of graphical effects: headers, lists, illustrations—whatever seems appropriate. In fact, you can have any HTML element within a form except another form.*

Text Form Field

Now that the form section of your document is defined, you can use the handy-dandy little Forms toolbar that has popped up. Each time you want to insert a text field, you can simply click on the Text Form Field button at top left, followed by the Options button at bottom left.

Form Field Options

Continue through the rest of the text fields you want to enter until your form looks somewhat like Figure 7-9. We've added text form fields for address and phone number. For each field, pick sensible limitations on the maximum length, but note that Word IA displays your defined fields as shaded areas that are never more than five characters wide regardless of your maximum length specification. When the user actually enters text, the shaded area expands as necessary up to the limit you defined. You can review (and re-edit) the options on any field you've already built by double-clicking on it, but the Name attribute may not appear to be correct in the Bookmark text box. It will be correct in the window you see when you choose Add Help Text and then the Help Key (F1) tag. Word IA makes use of these ready-made places to put hidden text because help text as such has no meaning in HTML.

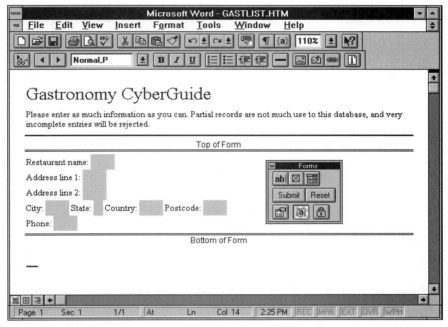

Figure 7-9: *All the primary text form fields are now in.*

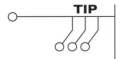

TIP

If at any time you find yourself with a form field right up against the left margin, you're going to have a little difficulty inserting text to its left. The answer is to select the field with your mouse, then use the left arrow key on your keyboard to position the edit cursor to the left of the field. Then you can type in the text you need.

A First Check of Your Form

To see if your form is operating correctly, click on the padlock icon (the Protect Form button) in the Forms toolbar to put your form temporarily in protected mode. Alternatively, you can switch to the Web Browse screen, which automatically protects the form. Note that there is no menu option for "Form Protect." Now you can no longer edit the form's text, but you can activate any of the fields with the mouse pointer or the Tab key, and verify that they limit entry to the number of characters that you specified. Doing a trial with this part of the form may suggest some layout improvements. When you're satisfied, click on the Protect Form button again to toggle protection off.

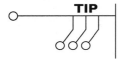

TIP

Any entries you make while checking your form in protected mode remain when you turn protection off. Simply protect it and unprotect it again to clear the content of all fields.

Creating a Drop–Down Form Field

Drop-down form fields give users the choice of several predefined options. In our restaurant form example, this would be highly appropriate for categorizing each restaurant in our database by the type of cuisine. Eventually we plan to make this into a searchable database, and cuisine, being an obvious search field, needs to be standardized.

1. Type the text to precede your box (**Cuisine:**), then click on the Drop-Down Form Field button in the Forms toolbar (it's at top right).

2. Click on the Form Field Options button. The Drop-Down Form Field Options dialog box appears.

3. Think of some options for your users to choose, but not too many. In our restaurant form, Italian, Chinese and Vegetarian are obvious ones, but there are many more, of course. Enter each option in the Drop-Down Item box and press Enter (or click on Add) to add it to the list. You can reorder the growing list at any time with the Move up/down arrow buttons. The first item on the list will be displayed as a default.

4. When you're done with your list, don't forget to enter the name attribute of this field in the Bookmark text box. (We entered **cuis**).

The item list is not cast in solid bronze: you can change its order, add to it or delete from it even after you have declared it done (just double-click on the field to bring back the dialog box). We picked 12 cuisine categories alphabetically, from American to Vegetarian plus Other—and Figure 7-10 shows this process half done.

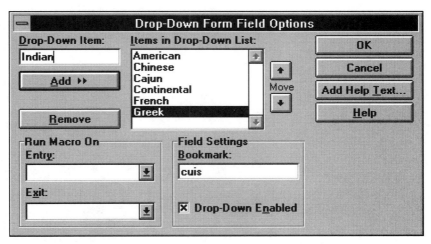

Figure 7-10: *The Drop-Down Form Field Options dialog box.*

When your list is complete, close the dialog box. You'll obviously want to see this magic work right away. Put the form in protected mode and click on your drop-down box. Satisfy yourself that you can pick anything from your item list and it stays there. If it doesn't, something's wrong; bring back the options box and recheck everything, especially that Drop-Down Enabled check box.

Optionally, you could now add a normal text form field labeled "Specify other:" on the same line. Here, people could enter options other than the ones in your drop-down field.

Using Default Text

In the drop-down form field example above, we noted that the first item you type in a list becomes the displayed default (it was fortuitous that American, being the first in alphabetical order, became our default cuisine style). We've continued our restaurant form by making another drop-down field for the price range Moderate/Expensive/Cheap/Rock bottom. We deliberately put Moderate first on the list because that's probably going to be the most common category, and users will not have to do anything to accept that default.

You can specify a default for a text field as well. What's the most common closing day for restaurants? Monday, of course. So now we create a text box for "Closing day(s):" and give it the name "closed" with a maximum length of 10 characters. Now we enter **Monday** into the special options box for Default text, and it's done. Once again, we've probably saved our users some keystrokes. At this point, our screen looks like Figure 7-11 (again, we've faked it by exposing both drop-down lists at once).

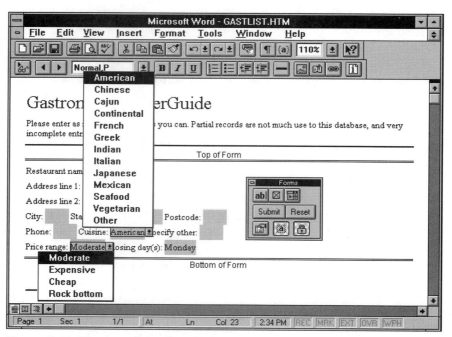

Figure 7-11: *The drop-down form fields in our restaurant questionnaire.*

Creating Check Boxes

Check boxes are the easiest kind of form field to create.

1. Enter the text to precede the box.

2. Click on the Check Box Form Field button in the Forms toolbar. Presto! A check box!

3. Click on Options and fill in a name attribute and a default (checked or unchecked), if you think it's appropriate.

Figure 7-12 shows the options box you get when you're inserting check box fields. Specify the size of the check boxes if you like, but be aware that this is not a recognized HTML attribute. It will affect the looks of your form only on the Word screen, not on a Web browser. You can also select a default value of Checked or Not Checked, and this attribute *is* recognized on the Web.

In our example, we've added check boxes for "Open for breakfast, lunch or dinner," and then for credit cards. We think lunch and dinner should default to checked; the others remain unchecked.

You'll need to protect the form to play with checking and unchecking the boxes.

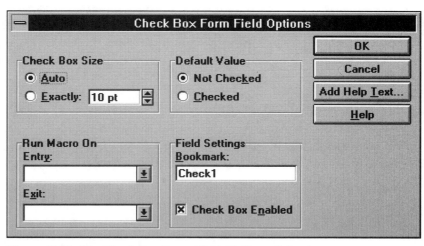

Figure 7-12: *The Check Box Form Field Options dialog box.*

Special Text Field Options

Take another look at the Text Field Options dialog box in Figure 7-7. You'll notice that there are some options we haven't yet explored. For Type, we've just used Regular Text. If you click on the drop-down list, you'll see that you can also allow for entering a number, a date, the current date or time, or a calculation. Each of these triggers an associated list of options in the Format drop-down list. For instance, if you choose Number in the Type box, then you can choose the format for your numbers (whole numbers, decimals and dollar format) in the Format drop-down. If you choose Date, you can specify the form in which you want the date to appear.

We're almost out of screen space on our restaurant form, but there's room for a few more special fields. Add the label "Number of tables:" and then a text field with length 3 and name "tables." Now look at the option list under Type in the dialog box and select Number. In the Number Format drop-down list, select 0. This procedure does not force your users to enter only numerals in this field, but it does guarantee that whatever they enter will be *evaluated* as a whole number by whatever program eventually accepts the data.

Finally, on this line, we've made one more text box and selected Current Date as the type. This creates a field that date-stamps every contribution to your restaurant database. If used locally, Word IA puts the date in automatically, but—alas—the Web has no such feature yet.

Creating Text Areas for Comments

You've certainly been getting the impression that creating form fields is a highly regimented process that constrains both you and your expected users quite tightly. In many ways, that's true—and for good reasons, mostly—but you can allow users to enter a great deal of free-form text. To create a box where the user can enter comments freely, follow these steps:

1. On a new line, enter **Comments:** (or whatever you want to label this box). Then create a text form field with the Text Form Field (*ab* |) button.

2. Select the Form Field Options button to bring up the options dialog box. Assign the Name for this field in the Bookmark box (in our example, cmts).

3. Click on Add Help Text.

4. Select the Status Bar tab.

5. Select the Type Your Own radio button.

6. In the text box, enter the size for your comments box in the form of *ROWS="#" COLS="#"* (where # is the number you want to specify).

We want to allow the users a nice big space where they can wax eloquent about the chocolate soufflé or pass on a tip about the Sunday specials or share with us any of the kinds of things that tend to break out of the bounds of defined form fields. We have to set *some* limits, but instead of assigning a maximum length to this field, we'll define a whole screen area 15 rows deep by 64 columns wide that users can rattle around in. Therefore, in the text window in Figure 7-13, we've entered **ROWS="15" COLS="64"**. Now OK everything, and you're done. What you've created is what HTML calls a TEXTAREA. You won't see it on this screen, but you'll see it later when we get to how this form looks in other Web browsers.

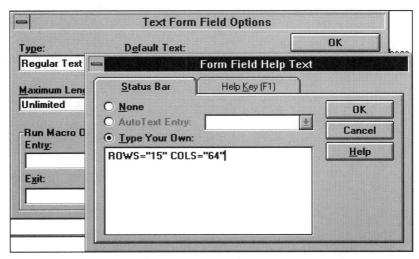

Figure 7-13: *Creating a whole screen area for free-form text entry.*

Submit & Reset Buttons

Well, we could all probably think of many other useful fields to put in an online restaurant questionnaire, but we've nearly filled the screen, and we've covered all the main field types (with the exception of radio buttons, which HTML allows for but Word IA doesn't display as such). It's time to think about the process of submitting the form.

On a new line, but still within the form delimiters, place the Submit button by clicking on it in the Forms toolbar. Up pops the (fairly scary) dialog box shown in Figure 7-14. Dealing with the easy part first, it should be intuitive that the Submit button has, by default, the word *Submit* written on it. If you want to change it to something more postmodern like "KEWL" or "Go for it, dude!" be our guest—just overwrite the boring old word *Submit* in the window provided. We'll just stick with the default, if it's OK with you. Post-mod has its place, but.... Well, let's just leave it at that.

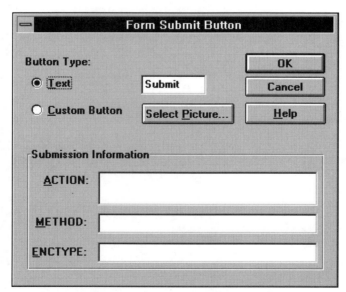

Figure 7-14: *Options for the process of submitting a completed form.*

The next artsy possibility is that we could dispense with words altogether and have a picture for users to punch when they've finished filling out the form. Browse the Web for awhile and you'll see plenty of these, some of them even in good taste! If you have something in mind—a picture of a nice roast duck might be fun here—have your picture handy in GIF format, pop the Custom Button radio button and go for the Select Picture option. Word IA will put you in the familiar file browse mode to go find that duck pic.

Now, about those nasty technical-looking text boxes labeled ACTION, METHOD and ENCTYPE. Together, they let you specify what happens to your data when somebody submits it. In the ACTION box, put the URL address where you want the data sent. This is normally the address of a data management program, specially written to handle your data. You probably need to ask your sysadmin to do this.

Now recall that every piece of data a user has entered into the form will be placed in a long string of name/value pairs. In the METHOD box we can either put **GET** (the default), which would mean that this data string is appended to the URL defined by ACTION, or **POST,** which would mean the data is sent on its way alone. You can pretty much ignore ENCTYPE—its intention is to allow some formatting of the data, but only one option is recognized by the Web right now, anyway.

It is considered polite to put a Reset button next to the Submit button. The Reset button clears the data from every form field and allows the user to start over (you'll need to be in the Web Browse screen to verify that your Reset button works). To include the Reset button, all you need to do is click on its likeness in the Forms toolbar. Unfortunately, you don't have the option of customizing this button (we've always wanted to create a Reset button out of a picture of Homer Simpson saying, "D'oh!"). But the form is finally, finally done. We've prettied ours up a bit, and we're ready to put it on the Web as shown in Figure 7-15, with the details of a restaurant we rather like all filled in.

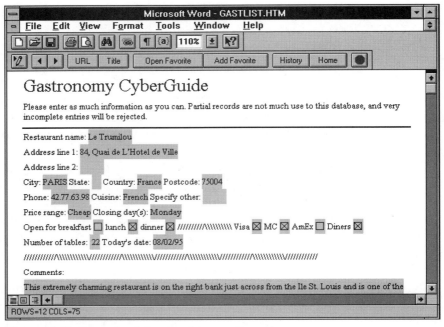

Figure 7-15: *Example of the complete questionnaire.*

Checking Your Form Online

If it seems anticlimactic to you to do all that work and then have to wait for some sysadmin to write a special program, here's a way to get instant gratification. The Netscape Web browser allows you to use a pseudo-URL, in the form of an e-mail address preceded by mailto: (there are no slashes involved). Do this:

1. **Enter mailto: in the ACTION box, followed immediately by your own e-mail address.**
2. **Enter POST in the METHOD box.**
3. **Save your file.**
4. **Connect to the Net.**

5. **Reopen the file as a local file in Netscape and fill in some data.**

6. **Send the file to yourself.**

Here's another idea. Put this in the ACTION box:

http://hoohoo.ncsa.uiuc.edu/htbin-post/post-query

Now connect to the Net and send some data. This very friendly site at the National Center for Supercomputing Applications is all set up to look at what you send and bang it right back to you in human-readable form. That's when the light bulb will go off in your head as you comprehend why we say, "make your Name attributes mean something."

Word IA Forms in Other Web Browsers

Figure 7-16 shows how the restaurant questionnaire we just created looks in Netscape, and it's about the same in Mosaic and InternetWorks, too. It's a bit of a shock because all our careful specifications of field widths seem to have been lost, and every field is 20 characters wide regardless.

Here's the problem: In HTML, form fields take two separate width attributes. One, the MAXLENGTH attribute, controls the maximum number of characters a user may enter into the field, and that's the one our numbers have been assigned to. But an entirely different attribute, SIZE="x", controls the width of the text box most browsers display. You can easily imagine that you might sometimes want a small screen box which allows quite a lot of text by scrolling horizontally as the user enters text. Word IA has no way to specify the SIZE attribute at all yet, and it isn't even possible to edit it in using the Html Hidden {a} button.

Here's the fix: Reopen your HTML document as text only (or open it in Notepad or some other simple text editor). Everywhere you see MAXLENGTH="x", add **SIZE="y"** manually. Generally, y is identical to x, but you may want to make y less than x. There certainly would be no point in making it larger than x because then you'd be creating a window larger than the largest possible input. Save your file and try again. Figure 7-17 shows the result of a few minutes work on our file. This time we've used the opportunity to do some promo for a restaurant that's *very* much closer to home. Figure 7-18 shows that big area we assigned for comments—and now you'll understand that those figures ROWS="15" COLS="64" were not just picked at random. We know from experience that they make a text area that fits comfortably into a single browser screen.

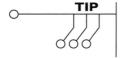

The SIZE="x" attribute has a different meaning if you assign it to a drop-down form field. In that case, it defines the number of list items that are on display at once. In Web page design, it's often desirable to have a scrolling list of 10 items that shows, say, four at a time. A rare but interesting gimmick is to give a drop-down field the attribute MULTIPLE SIZE="x". This makes it possible for the user to select more than one item from a list that is displayed x items at a time. However, Word IA does not support this style and is liable to turn your multiple-choice list into a series of check boxes.

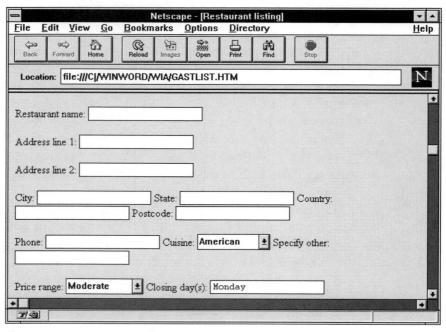

Figure 7-16: *Top half of the form as it first looks in Netscape.*

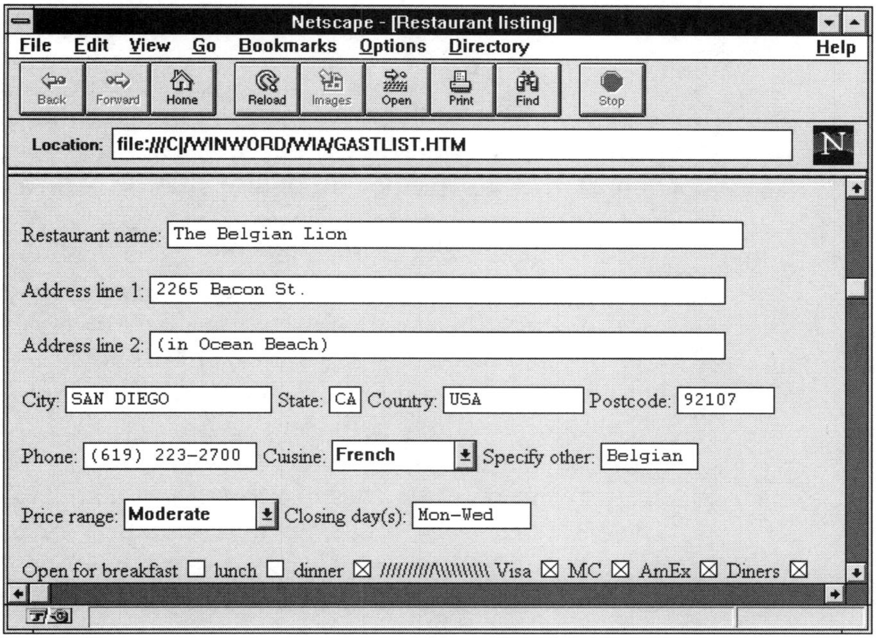

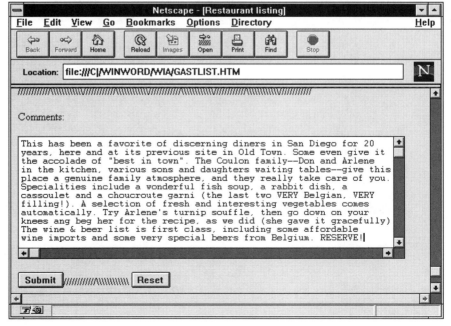

Figure 7-17: *Form field widths adjusted appropriately.*

Figure 7-18: *The text area that was defined in Figure 7-13.*

The Common Gateway Interface (cgi)

Like most everything on the Internet, the Web depends on the client-server relationship. The *client* (that's you—or your desktop computer) is capable of a lot of user-friendly stuff such as displaying the attractive and useful hypertext pages we're now getting used to. When it comes to connecting to the real world, however, the client depends on the much greater computing power of a *server.* There's already a trend to bring the power of a server to PC- or (especially) Mac-type machines, but for now the likelihood is that your server is a far more capable machine, running software you wouldn't want to comprehend.

Therein lies the difficulty of describing how to follow through with advanced HTML files like forms and searchable indexes. The type of database you might want to build up with a restaurant lister like the one we just described is assumed to be in the server—most likely a UNIX computer. The interface between a user hitting the Submit button on an HTML form and the database itself is managed via the so-called Common Gateway Interface (cgi), a standard for packaging and formatting requests like those name/value pairs. These cgi programs are scripts written in programming languages like C or Perl.

Since Word IA's own help screens palm you off with language like "...you need to work with your Web administrator...," we're going to take the cue and regard cgi scripting as beyond the scope of this book. After all, if you decided to just go with Netscape's mailto: option and arranged for everyone's restaurant listings to arrive in your e-mail box encoded as name/value pairs, you'd have the information. But you'd still have to figure out a way to make use of it, and that would be the subject of a different book.

Sensitive Maps

Another common task for cgi scripts is to manage user-generated requests from what's sometimes called a *sensitive map.* Flip back to Figure 4-7 and you'll see that Sensitive Map is an option in the

Advanced Insert Picture dialog box that we glossed over at the time. A sensitive map, of course, is a map of the world that leaves out all the disputed boundaries because it doesn't want to hurt anyone's feelings.

Just kidding. For the *real* story on sensitive maps, look at Figure 7-19. A sensitive map is not always a map in the common sense of the word, but in this case it is—the figure shows one part of SUNY Buffalo's Virtual Tourist service. It's all one big picture, but different areas of it are hyperlinks to different destinations. In this case, each destination is an information page about an area of the world.

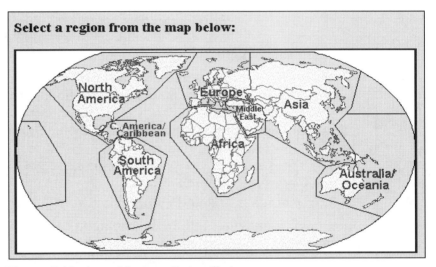

Figure 7-19: *A sensitive map that really is a map.*

It's easy enough to illustrate how a sensitive map works from the user's point of view, but less easy to explain how to create and implement one.

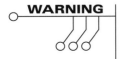

The following section contains material that some readers may find mathematical in nature. If the words coordinate *and* circumference *strike terror into your heart, skip it. Sensitive maps are not for you.*

Sensitive Maps: A Primer

The principle of creating sensitive maps—also known as *active images*—is not hard to grasp. Each area of an image that you want to make into a hyperlink has to be defined by x,y coordinates, measured in pixels from an origin at the top left corner of the picture. An "area" may be any one of the following:

- a rectangle, defined by its top left and bottom right corners
- a circle, defined by its center and any point on its circumference
- an irregular shape, defined by a series of up to 100 vertex coordinates
- a single point

Figure 7-19, as you can see, has no easy circles or rectangles. All active areas on a sensitive map must be defined, associated with a hyperlink destination in a data file and listed in a data file called the *image map*. At the Buffalo site, the entry for South America in this file is actually

```
poly (109,139) (110,153) (150,242) (176,235)
(201,143)(161,118)(132,119)
http://wings.buffalo.edu/world/sam.html
```

Clicking anywhere within the heptagon defined by those vertex coordinates would link to the file sam.html at the specified URL, and the same goes for all the other geographical areas. An extra line in the image map beginning "default" specifies what happens if a user clicks on the picture but outside any defined active area (in this case, it takes the user to a list of Web servers).

So to enhance your Web site, you can now use any of the helper applications listed in the sidebar "Further Resources on Sensitive Mapping" to create a sensitive map. Scan in that picture of the family on the beach and have fun deciding what happens if you click on granpaw's bald head!

The hyperlink destination you need to enter in the Insert Image dialog box as you bring the picture into your page does not point to any of the final destinations involved. Instead, it's a pointer to the image map defining the sensitive areas of that picture, but having got that far you really will need some help from your sysadmin! The problem is that you cannot install and test the picture plus its associated image map without having the server software and a specially made database to interpret your intentions.

Further Resources on Sensitive Mapping
A program that allows you to define sensitive areas with your mouse, by Thomas Boutell, can be found at
  ftp://sunsite.unc.edu/pub/packages/infosystems/
  WWW tools/mapedit
Interactive mapping of images that are already on the Web is made into an ingenious game at
  http://www.tns.lcs.mit.edu/cgi-bin/mapmaker
And finally, Luke Duncan of Ventana Online (our publisher's online products department) has an explanatory page with links to more and more detail, at
  http://blake.oit.unc.edu/~duncan/mapex.html

The World of Hypermedia

In all this talk about hypertext and the things you can do with it, we've nearly overlooked one of the most exciting frontiers in the world of electronic publishing: the world of hypermedia. Hypermedia gives you the ability to insert both audio and video files into your text so that you can click on a link just as you would to jump to a new text file. But instead of displaying a text file, you play back a prerecorded audio segment or even a short movie clip.

Both of these art forms are in their infancy on the Web, and the main reason is that it takes considerable time to download audio and video files of any significant size, and considerable computer space to store them. But we'd be remiss if we didn't at least touch on the subject—especially since Word IA makes it as easy to insert audio and video files as it is to insert any hyperlink. Even small files can add a nice extra touch to your Web page.

Inserting Audio Files

Of the two forms of hypermedia available in Webspace, audio is the most accessible to your average Joe Webauthor. In fact, creating an audio file and inserting it into your Web page can be incredibly simple and quite inexpensive.

There are just three things you need, if you don't already have them:

※ a sound card with the appropriate software

※ speakers

※ a microphone

If your computer came equipped with all of the above—and many do, these days—you already have everything you need. If not, you can get the microphone for as little as $10, the speakers for as little as $20 and the sound card—well, it depends how fancy you want to get. But suffice it to say the whole kit needn't cost you more than $100, and you can plug it all in yourself.

If you've got the sound card, you can use the Sound Recorder that comes with Windows (you'll need to install the appropriate drivers), but you'll have more sophisticated editing capabilities with software that comes with a sound card like Sound Blaster.

Make your recording first and save it, following the instructions with your software. To insert your audio file into an HTML document you've created:

1. Place your cursor at the point where you want to insert the audio file. Select the text to use as a hyperlink anchor.

2. Click on the Hyperlink button (or choose Insert/Hyperlink from the File menu).

3. Enter or edit the anchor text in the Text box.

4. To associate a sound icon or image with the file, use the Image button and choose the image file.

5. In the File Name box, enter the name of the sound file, or select it by browsing your directories. You'll need to select All Files in the File Type box to see files with sound extensions.

6. Choose OK.

The file will be inserted as a hyperlink. To test your link, double-click on the link text or sound icon (which will automatically switch you to Web Browse View), or switch to Web Browse View and click on the hyperlink. The sound file is an *embedded object*—meaning that Word will launch the appropriate application to deal with it when selected. You'll get an icon on your screen that looks like a surprise package. See Figure 7-20. You can either

≫ double-click on the icon to activate the file, or

≫ click on the right mouse button while the cursor is on the object to see options. Among the options are Play Sound—obviously what we want to do—and Edit Sound, which activates the Sound Recorder to allow you to edit.

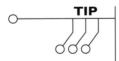

TIP

If you're using a sound application other than the Windows Sound Recorder, your options may be Activate Contents Package (which in this case means simply "play it, Sam") and Edit Package Package, a stuttery bit of nonsense, but we get it.

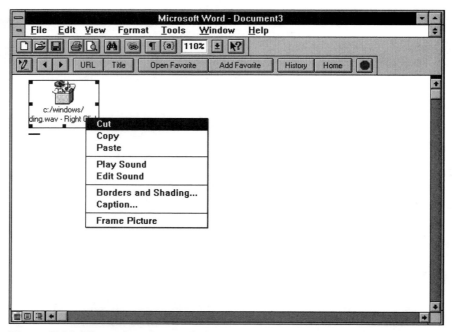

Figure 7-20: *The package icon indicates an embedded object; clicking on the right mouse button gives you some options.*

If your file doesn't play and instead you get a message saying that there's no application associated with the file, check that the Windows File Manager knows what application to launch. Choose File/Associate and type the file extension (e.g., .wav). Then select the application you have for playing audio files (e.g., Sound Recorder).

Audio files in Web documents are often signalled with the insertion of an audio icon or button, which makes it clear to the viewer that the link is to an audio file. This prevents users who don't have audio capabilities from wasting their time trying to download something they won't be able to appreciate. A variety of sound buttons and icons are available by FTP at several online icon libraries. It's also polite to give users some idea of the file size, so they can take account of their own computer capacity and modem speed before trying to download the file.

In Figure 7-21, you can see how the Smithsonian Institution has added both a sound and a video clip from the Secretary of the Institution, with all the essential information users need.

Figure 7-21: *Audio and video files are clearly indicated on the Smithsonian Institution's Web page.*

About Audio

Audio files come in a variety of types, with extensions like .wav, .au, .voc, .aif, .mid, .cmf and .snd. The Windows Sound Recorder will make and play only .wav files, which are fine for most applications. If you're an audiophile and want to get fancy, you should get an independent sound software package. For just playing sound files, you can play just about any type of sound you come across with an application called WPLANY (short for We Play Anything). You can get it by FTP at ftp.cam.org/systems/ms-windows/slip-ppp/VIEWERS

Inserting Video Files

Creating and manipulating video files is a step more complicated than the relatively simple business of audio files. While you can make simple audio files with the standard Windows accessories, you need several powerful software applications if you want to play Walt Disney on the Web. You'll also need some pretty state-of-the-art computer equipment, including a good-sized hard drive and high-speed CD-ROM. The technology for all of this is changing rapidly, but at the moment the speed and storage capacity of today's home computers are not adequate for making and playing high-quality, synchronized sound-and-video files. However, anyone who says it isn't possible should be prepared to eat his or her words in just a few years.

It's beyond the scope of this book to explain how to make videos, but suffice it to say there are some pretty good applications available for making computerized animation files, and the technology is evolving so fast it's hard to keep up with it. What you can do depends on how big your ambitions are and what you want to spend. Macintosh hardware is the preferred computer platform for moviemaking applications, although some applications are available for Windows.

Before you get carried away, though, let's explain what's involved. The complete do-it-yourself moviemaker who wants to make an animated movie with a home computer needs to learn to use up to 30 different software packages. One recommendation is that you'll need at least 250mb for your programs alone. Then there are the files themselves. For a live-action movie, you're advised to have 100mb of external disk storage for each minute of the finished movie.

Move Over, Mr. DeMille
A good, up-to-date guide to the state of the art in computer moviemaking can be found at the Homeport Hollywood Web site at this address:
http://www.el-dorado.ca.us/~homeport/
Here you'll find reviews of all the latest software, advice on both hardware and software and back issues of the *Digital Movie News*, which contains tons of useful references for would-be computer moviemakers.

ATI Technologies Video-It! is a new product that lets you capture video from a video source and edit it on your computer for presentation. Get information about this product at this address:
http://www.atitech.ca/multi/index.html

A more accessible bit of technology for simple video inserts for Web presentation is software that allows you to capture video from a video source such as a VCR, video camera, laser disc or television, then compress it and edit it on your computer screen. (The frame speed still makes this of rather jerky quality, but it has its uses.) If your computer equipment isn't up to this and you have a one-time need for a video clip, you can easily have the conversion done professionally.

Once you have your video file, inserting it into your document is simple. It's inserted as a hyperlink just like a sound file, or like any hyperlink, for that matter. The only difference is in how you choose to identify it. Just as with audio files, you need to clearly signal a link to a video file since a lot of users won't have movie viewers and won't want to waste their time. (Movie icons are also available at icon libraries.) And it's even more important that you include the size of the file, since these files can take quite awhile to download. Most users prefer to set their preference to Save when downloading a video file so that they'll be able to replay it and add it to their collections rather than just play it once on the fly.

To insert a video file, follow the instructions we gave above for inserting a hyperlink to an audio file. The most common file types are .qtw (for QuickTime) and .mpg (for movies of the MPEG type). Word IA lets you create a link to movie files, but you won't be able to follow the link and launch your movie player from within Word IA. If you have the right movie player application, you'll be able to test the link and play the video from within another Web browser.

Movie Viewers
While making movies might be beyond your scope, movie viewers are not at all complicated to install and use, and they are quite easy to find on the Net. QuickTime is available by FTP for $9.95 from the Apple FTP site. For information on how to order and download it, go to this address:
    http://quicktime.apple.com
For movies of the MPEG type, try MPEGPLAY. It's available at
    ftp://gatekeeper.dec.com/pub/micro/msdos/win3/desktop
The files are
    mpegwin.zip for Windows 3.1
    mpegw32g.zip for Windows NT/Windows 95

Moving On

We've covered some pretty powerful Web publishing tools in this chapter. If you've tried some of these things as you read, you should be feeling pretty smart and just about ready for graduation.

We still have a few more tricks up our sleeves, though. In the next chapter, we'll let you in on some of the more advanced tips and tricks that Web authors use—things like interlaced and transparent GIFs, as well as special design features that take advantage of the HTML 3 tags that Netscape can display. When you're all done polishing your Web pages with the tricks that appeal to you, we'll tell you how to assemble your masterpiece and get ready to post it on the Web.

8

Tips & Tricks

If you've cruised the Web at all with another Web browser, especially with Netscape, you've undoubtedly noticed some things on Web pages that aren't in any book you've seen or any reference guide to HTML you've perused. Part of the reason is that some of the tricks you see are not really kosher—that is, they don't stick to the rigid specifications of HTML 2 that have been internationally agreed upon, to which Word IA soberly confines itself.

In this chapter, we'll tell you how they do some of those fancy design tricks—some of which are perfectly legitimate but simply require a little technical expertise or the right software, and some of which are just free-wheeling fun. You can pick among them to suit your own attitude.

Inserting HTML Markup Tags

As linguists are fond of reminding us, language is not static, but constantly evolving. It should come as no surprise, then, that at six years of age HTML is still evolving, as are most of the HTML editing programs making the scene these days. Word IA's debut version is based on the accepted codes in HTML 2, but there's every reason to believe that as HTML marches on, so will Word IA.

To account for change, Word IA's designers have made it possible for you to use HTML tags other than the ones conveniently available on your toolbars and menus. That includes a few recognized HTML 2 tags that Word IA, for arcane reasons, has not incorporated. Then there are tags that are recognized by certain Web browsers and not others. Some of these tags are part of the evolving HTML 3 specifications. Others have been initiated by adventurous designers and, while they may never be generally accepted, are nonetheless part of the kit you can use.

You can insert any valid HTML tag in Word IA using the Html Markup option on the Insert menu. When you choose this option, you get the dialog box shown in Figure 8-1. In the figure, we're in the process of inserting one of the most useful HTML 2 tags that Word IA does not include in its usual menu options. That's the <BR> tag, which signals a line break without triggering the usual extra spacing that a paragraph break gives. This can be very useful when you're aligning text to a picture but want only part of a line next to the graphic, or when you want a new line for something like an address or a short list but want single spacing.

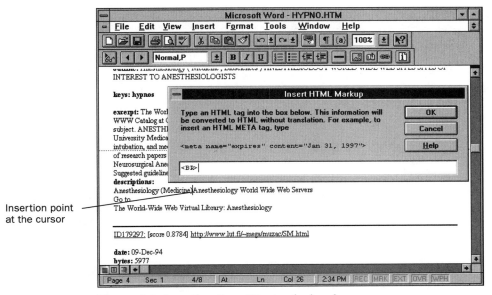

Figure 8-1: *Inserting the <BR> tag by hand.*

Simply type your HTML tag in the text box provided. Note that all HTML tags are enclosed within angle brackets. You must use the HTML Markup command to insert HTML tags. If you tried to type an angle bracket directly into your document, Word IA would convert it to a character entity (<).

Even though Word IA doesn't give you the option of inserting the <BR> tag any other way, it still recognizes it and will treat it correctly, as it does all HTML 2 tags. You'll find a list of all the valid HTML 2 tags in Appendix B. Some additional tags whose display is entirely browser-dependent are given later in this chapter.

When you enter a tag that is not recognized by Word IA, Word IA initially displays it in the HTML Edit View as <<HTML Markup>>. You can double-click that notation to reveal the text of the markup in the HTML Markup dialog. After you close and reopen the file, it is displayed as <<Unknown HTML Tag>>. When you switch to Web Browse View this notation disappears, and any text you've entered between HTML tags is displayed normally. The Web browser simply ignores anything it's not capable of displaying.

Meta Tags & Other Advanced Options

When you open the Insert HTML Markup dialog (described above and shown in Figure 8-1), the example you're given is a *meta tag*. Meta tags simply give information about your document, similar to what you see in the Summary Info box on the standard Word File menu. If you open your file as Text Only, you will probably see two meta tags that Word IA has added to your document:

```
<META NAME="GENERATOR" CONTENT="Internet
Assistant for Word 1.0Z">
<META NAME="AUTHOR" CONTENT="Joe Webauthor">
```

All meta tags appear between the <HEAD>. . .</HEAD> tags of your document, which come before the <BODY>. . .</BODY> elements that define the content of your document. The meta tag information does not affect the display of your document in a Web browser; it is seen only if the user chooses to reveal source code.

Word IA allows you to insert three other useful elements in the HEAD portion of your document: Base URL, Next ID and Is Index. To access these, choose the HTML Document Info option on the File menu, then the Advanced button, which brings up the dialog box shown in Figure 8-2.

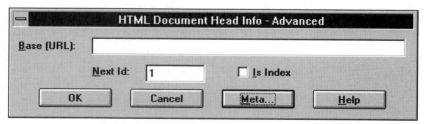

Figure 8-2: *The HTML Document Head Info - Advanced dialog box.*

Base URL

In normal circumstances, you would post your document and all its related documents together on one computer or network, and in all likelihood they would stay that way. But what happens if you move your home page to another location—say to a different computer or a different drive on your network, and you don't move the documents that are linked to it?

Obviously, you can go back and redo all your links. But another solution, and one less prone to error, is to specify a base URL. Simply specify the original location of your document as the base URL. Then all relative links within your document will be referred to that address first. Think of it as mail forwarding.

Next Id

Next Id is used by automatic hypertext editors to keep track of documents created in the editing process. It is not meant to be used by human authors, nor is it interpreted by the Web browser. You might enable this if, for instance, you had a document that was designed to change daily or on some regular basis through an automatic program.

Is Index

The Is Index element informs the Web browser that the document is an index document—the user interface to a searchable database. Documents containing ISINDEX elements are usually handled by server gateway programs designed for database searches, and the user is presented with a query to search a database by keyword. This is not the same as a "find" operation on a document on your screen. The ISINDEX attribute would normally be added to a document through the server-side program that created it, and manual addition of ISINDEX is not normally recommended.

Advanced Design Features With Netscape

Back in Chapter 3 we referred to the <BLINK>. . .</BLINK> tags that make things blink on Netscape screens but that other browsers disdain (look back at Figure 3-14 to refresh your memory). Many Netscape-compliant home pages are flashy in both the literal and metaphorical senses! Blinking text is not the only gimm..., er, feature Netscape came up with, either; a complete list of the so-called Netscape extensions will follow shortly, but the highlights are as follows:

- blocks of text beside pictures
- horizontal rules of varying length and width

❧ patterned and colored backgrounds

❧ font size changes at will

One view of these capabilities is that they are useful and fun, and they enhance page design in important ways. So what if they're not universally recognized? As long as the use of these *spécialités de la maison* doesn't actually detract from page presentation in other browsers, no harm done. Perhaps the slumbering dinosaur that is the Internet Engineering Task Force (IETF) will eventually catch up, realize that these options are necessary and adopt them as standards.

Another position is that, even if some of these things are useful—OK, perhaps even necessary—it's best for manufacturers to wait for established standards. It's like one corporation coming out with a flashy and popular new light bulb that doesn't fit the US standard screw receptacle, they say.

And although the Netscape extension tags are transparent in other browsers, they tempt hot HTML designers to show off their skill with the latest codes, making pages that become dull in other browsers and that many Web professionals think are in bad taste, anyway. One critic, Lar Kaufman of Polymedia Services, recently wrote in a posting to a professional maillist that such things "violate the fundamental purpose of [the Web], that of universally accessible, portable documentation."

As for ourselves, we regularly use the ALIGN=LEFT attribute for pictures now in our pages (and we even recommended it to improve Figure 6-10 of this book), but we always cross-check the appearance of the page in a non-Netscape browser. We've even been known to make things blink—once in a while.

Fun Times on the Web

There's a lot of talk about what a hostile, nasty place the Net can be—it's full of people who flame newbies and delight in spoiling the fun. Personally, we can easily ignore the hostility and have come, in fact, to enjoy the wry techno-humor that is just as much a feature of the Net as is hostility.

The dispute over the Netscape extensions is a case in point. We love to visit the Enhanced for Netscape Hall of Shame page, where Chris Pearce regularly nominates some pages as examples of egregious overuse of the special codes and others, conversely, for proclaiming to be Netscape-compliant because they enjoy the cachet when, in reality, they use no extended codes. Figure 8-3 shows one of the former. Chris's page is at this URL:

http://www.europa.com/~yyz/netbin/netscape_hos.html

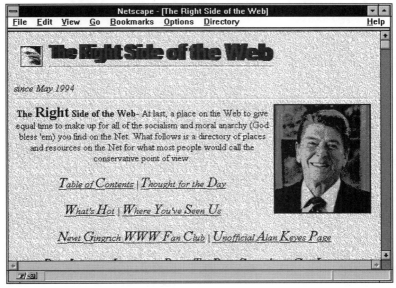

Figure 8-3: *A political page that was voted into the Hall of Shame.*

And then there's the very witty Stupid Netscape Tricks page by John Leavitt, which allows you to enter the URL of your own traditional, boring page and have it randomly enhanced by things that flash and fonts that bounce. John can turn a technical description of a widget into something that looks like a ransom note in seconds (see Figure 8-4). This fun page is at the following address (note the rare use of an http port number other than 80):

http://thule.mt.cs.cmu.edu:8001/tools/nutscape

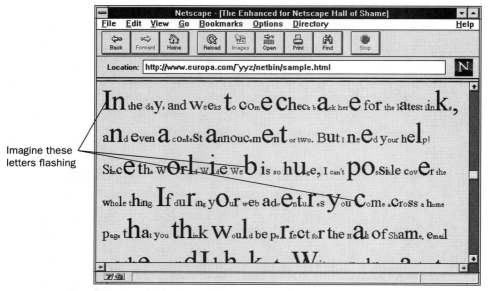

Imagine these letters flashing

Figure 8-4: *The Hall of Shame page text, after going through the Nutscape treatment.*

Font Crazy!
The new FONT tag has caused a bigger brouhaha than perhaps any other Netscape extension. Fonts that change six times in the course of a single word do indeed violate all known rules of typesetting. But then, so does *Wired* magazine, which has now established itself as a leader in avant-garde design. And when sans-serif type was first introduced, in Switzerland, it was dubbed *grotesk* because it looked so ugly. Humankind, it seems, is typographically conservative by nature.

Netscape Extensions

Netscape Extension	Description
<IMG ALIGN=left, etc.>	The text alignment attributes left, right, texttop, absmiddle, baseline and absbottom have been added to the conventional choices of top, middle and bottom. The left and right alignments are particularly useful in flowing text around images, and anticipate HTML 3 conventions.
<IMG WIDTH=w HEIGHT=h>	Define the size of the image in pixels and, if used, save the time normally needed by the client software to calculate them.
<IMG VSPACE=v HSPACE=h>	Specify that text may not approach the picture closer than v and h pixels vertically and horizontally.
<IMG BORDER=x>	Allows HTML authors to specify a colored border around an image, of thickness x pixels. It also affects the width of any border that might be present anyway, signifying that the image is a hyperlink. As a collateral, BORDER=0 would inhibit a hyperlink border.
<FONT SIZE=x>text</FONT>	May be applied to a section of text, controlling its font size in arbitrary units from 1 to 7 with a default of 3.
<BASEFONT SIZE=x>	Allows authors to specify the base font size of an entire document, in the same arbitrary units as above. Within the document, font sizes may be specified *relative* to the base, as $+x$ or $-x$. →

Netscape Extension	Description
<BODY BACKGROUND= "wallpapr.gif">	Causes an image to be tiled into the background of the entire document. The user can elect not to be exposed to this wanton excess by setting background preferences in his or her own Web browser to override the author's.
<BODY BGCOLOR= "#rrggbb">	Color of the page background is specified with a hexadecimal string (rrggbb) controlling red, green and blue components of the color. (Appendix D contains a list of these strings, translated into designer terms like "lemon chiffon" and "peachpuff3.")
<BODY TEXT="#rrggbb">	Controls the color of nonlinking text.
<BODY LINK="#rrggbb">	Controls the color of link text.
<BODY ALINK="#rrggbb">	Controls the color of active links.
<BODY VLINK="#rrggbb">	Controls the color of visited links.
<CENTER>text</CENTER>	Applied to a line of text, this causes it to be displayed centered between the current margins.
<BR CLEAR=left>	Breaks a line and does not restart it until the left margin is clear of images. The attribute "right" does the same thing with the right margin, and "all" inspects both margins.
<NOBR>text text text </NOBR>	Inhibits line breaks between the tags. If the text is longer than the screen width, the line just goes on, and on, and on....
<WBR>	Functions as a "soft" word-break guide, and also within a <NOBR> section to mean "if you really must break, do it here."
<HR>	The classical <HR> element has been made baroque by the addition of some attributes of its own:
<HR SIZE=n>	Horizontal rule, *n* pixels thick (2 is the standard).

Netscape Extension	Description
<HR WIDTH=n>	Horizontal rule, *n* pixels wide (600 is full-screen width).
<HR WIDTH=p%>	Horizontal rule whose width is a percentage of full-screen width.
<HR ALIGN=left/right/center>	Aligns a horizontal rule left, right or center, as specified.
<HR NOSHADE>	Creates a solid black line.
List Options	Options have been added for the creators of bulleted and numbered lists to play with. In a conventional bulleted list, the bullets are rendered as solid discs, then open circles, then squares as you progress down the levels of indention. Variations include:
<UL TYPE=disc/circle/square>	Allows bullet style to be specified by the author.
<OL TYPE=A/a/I/i>	Has the effect of replacing the conventional numbers in a numbered list with uppercase letters/lowercase letters/large roman numerals/small roman numerals.
<LI TYPE=disc/circle/square>	Controls the style of bulleting of individual list items.
<LI VALUE=n>	Resets the count of a numbered list, so that listings can change in midstream!

Table 8-1: *Netscape extensions and their meanings.*

In addition to the special extensions in Table 8-1, Netscape has gone ahead and implemented all of the table creation codes still under consideration by IETF. We go into these in more detail under "Table Tricks With HTML 3" later in this chapter.

HTML authors who like decoration have already discovered that they can make use of the <TABLE BORDER> tag to create a fancy border around page elements like inline pictures. They simply define them as a table having only one cell (there's an example of this technique on the Netscape Hall of Shame page).

In Netscape, complete documents can now be embedded within Web pages. We could embed this whole chapter (the file 8trix.doc), written in Word 6.0, within a Web page using this code:

<EMBED SRC="8trix.doc">

So long as the user also has Word 6.0 and has set file associations in the Windows File Manager to associate .doc files with Word, the whole thing will unfold into the Web page with its Word formatting intact. In fact, that is exactly how we made Figure 8-5. It's a part of this chapter's original text, including some of the input from our editor, Lynn Jaluvka, embedded in an HTML file. Notice how the Word 6.0 screen is wrapped inside the Netscape screen. (In order to do this for real, our .doc file would have to be on the server, of course.) Another demo of the EMBED tag is at this address:

http://home.netscape.com/assist/net_sites/embed_tag.html

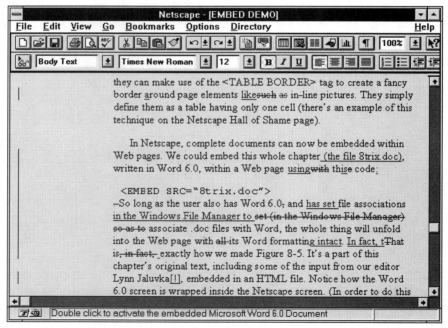

Figure 8-5: *Part of the text of this chapter, embedded in a Netscape HTML document.*

Finally, Netscape's seemingly tireless programmers have come up with a convention that they call a *dynamic document*. This is a way to make one document automatically load another after a time delay. The second document could obviously be arranged to load a third, and so on, creating what's been called a "poor man's animation." The code that makes a document dynamic belongs in the <HEAD>. . .</HEAD> section, and might look like this:

```
<META HTTP-EQUIV="Refresh" CONTENT="2; URL=http://
www.thegroup.net/kidder/anim2.htm">
```

That code says that after two seconds the document anim2.htm should be loaded; anim2 will then load anim3; and so on. Netscape has all sorts of suggestions about games you might play with this, at this address:

http://home.netscape.com/assist/net_sites/dynamic_docs.html

How You Can Play Along

Word IA will presumably implement HTML 3 conventions as they come along, but it's unlikely that it will support Netscape's high jinks. However, there's no need to deprive yourself of the thrill of seeing your pages pulsate or your list numbering change in mid-list if that kind of thing turns you on. You have a choice of three ways to insert special HTML coding into your documents:

- Use the Insert/HTML Markup menu option to insert code at the cursor, as explained in "Inserting HTML Markup Tags" at the beginning of this chapter.

- Close your HTML file and reopen it with the Confirm Conversions check box selected in the Open dialog box, then convert the file as Text Only. You are then working directly in the source code.

- Use a simple text editor such as Notepad to edit your source code.

Happy flashing, bouncing and embedding!

Table Tricks With HTML 3

If a lot of the Netscape extensions sound unnecessary for your Web requirements, there's something else in HTML 3 that's much in demand and not much in dispute. That's the need for elements to define tables. The specifications are already pretty much agreed upon by the gurus in charge, and several browsers besides Netscape already support table elements, including the next-most-popular Web browser, NCSA Mosaic 2.0. (InternetWorks does not.)

In Chapter 6, "Converting Word Documents to HTML," we talked about converting tables you've created in Word to HTML. You saw how certain elements, such as borders and heads, don't convert. If you're comfortable with Word tables and are satisfied with the results, you can, of course, choose to use that method; your tables will be perfectly readable on the Web. But if you long for something more—border, boxes, different size cells, special alignments (in short, a little glitz to brighten up your data doldrums)—HTML 3's tables are for you.

You can create your table as a separate file and then insert it in the main document when you're done, or you can start right out creating it in your main file.

- If you're starting fresh, open a new file using the HTML template. Give your document a title using the Title button, and enter any initial text you wish to include before starting your table. Then save your file, close it and reopen it as Text Only.

- If you're inserting the table in an existing HTML file, open your file as a Text Only file.

To start your table, insert the tag <TABLE>. If you want a border around the table and boxes within it, use <TABLE BORDER>. Add a few empty lines and then insert the table end element, </TABLE>. Make sure that the start and end table tags are between the start and end body tags, <BODY>. . .</BODY>. All of your table information will go between the table tags. We put the HTML tags in uppercase to distinguish them from the text, and to match Word IA's convention, but in fact HTML tags can be in either uppercase or lowercase.

The next logical element to define is the caption. The table caption is the title of your table, which in most browsers appears above the table. Put the caption between the tags <CAPTION> . . .</CAPTION> on a separate line.

The three elements that go to define your table and the attributes that can be included with them are as follows:

- *<TH ALIGN=left>head</TH>*—This element defines a Table Header—the head for a row or column. The header may be aligned left, right or center. To be perfectly proper the table header should have an end tag, </TH>, but if you don't include it, it will be assumed by the next TH, TR or TD tag. There are two other attributes that can be defined with the TH tag:

  - *ROWSPAN=n*—Specifies how many table rows are spanned by the table header cell. If you do not include this attribute, the default will be 1.

  - *COLSPAN=n*—Specifies how many table columns are spanned by the table header cell. The default is 1.

- *<TR>*—Indicates the end of a table row.

- *<TD>data</TD>*—Specifies a table data cell.

We used all these tags and attributes to make the table you see in Figure 8-6. The beginning of the text file that created it is shown in Figure 8-7. To make it less confusing, we've left out the empty cells <TD>.</TD> (13 times to make each row), but note that in order to make it draw a box around each cell we had to enter something, so we've used a period.

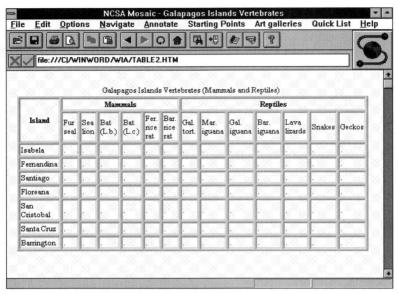

Figure 8-6: *Mosaic 2.0 demonstrates the use of HTML 3's Table elements.*

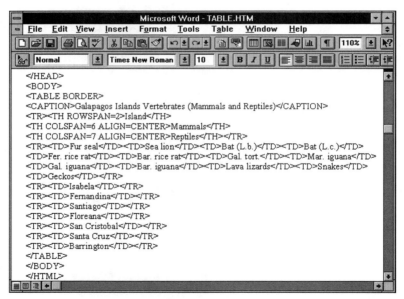

Figure 8-7: *The coding for this page may look complicated, but there are only five main HTML tags involved.*

Now for some practical advice: it's helpful to use Word IA to create your initial HTML document because all of the initial HTML tags are created for you, including the BODY and HEAD elements. But once you get down to the nitty gritty of creating your table manually, you'll find it a lot easier to work in a straight text editor. The reason is that you'll want to be checking your work as you go, trying out what you're doing by loading it into Netscape or Mosaic or whatever Web browser you have that supports tables.

Word is very jealous of its documents and won't allow you to open a file in another program while it's still open in Word. Text editors like Windows Notepad (perfectly adequate for the task, though it doesn't wrap text) are much more *laissez faire* and allow you to do what you like with the file while it floats in editing limbo. To see the effect of what you've done while editing, save the file before switching to your Web browser, then use the Reload button to load the latest edited version.

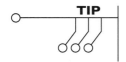

TIP

Once you start entering data in your table, it's easy to get lost in a forest of coding. So if your need for table-making is heavy, you'd be well advised to get a software program that makes this easier. LaTeX is one popular one.

After you've edited your table, don't even try to view it in Word IA as an HTML file unless you can bear the scolding it gives you about all the "Unknown HTML tags." You won't be able to make sense of it in Word IA at all. For that reason, if you intend to insert your table into another HTML document you've created in Word IA, be sure you've completely finished editing the document first. Alternatively, you can insert a hyperlink to your table rather than the table itself.

There are so many varieties of tables that we can't possibly cover them all here. For an excellent primer on using the Table elements, take a look at Netscape's online document The Table Sampler at this URL:

http://home.netscape.com/assist/net_sites/tables.html

Improving Your Image

Everybody involved in Web publishing assumes that, like everything else, the Web will keep on improving until we reach—or at least approach very closely—the ideal of a lavishly illustrated page that will appear instantaneously on the user's screen with the quality and immediacy of a new page in a glossy magazine. Then we'll all look back on the good old days of the '90s and chortle as we remember how crude everything was, and how many hours of our precious time were wasted waiting for pages to load.

Since this ideal is still a way off, it's incumbent upon Web authors and publishers to help the users out in any way they can. Even with the steam-age technology we have to live with right now, there are ways to manipulate images that can enhance the Web cruising experience for users.

Interlaced GIFs

We've already mentioned that nothing slows down a page more than thoughtlessly designed inline GIF images, and we've given you a couple of tips on speeding things up. Here's one that doesn't actually speed loading of a GIF, but makes the process more interesting and so, perhaps, creates the *illusion* of speed.

You may have noticed that the pictures on some Web sites appear first in very crude, almost unrecognizable form, then take on more and more detail until they are finally done. Figure 8-8 shows the four stages in the development of the Exploratorium's banner, which uses this technique, called *interlacing*. If you think of the GIF image as being composed of scan lines like a TV picture, interlacing is not hard to understand. Instead of delivering lines $1,2,3,4...n$ one after the other, like a conventional GIF, a four-pass interlaced GIF delivers lines $1,5,9,13...n$ and then goes back to the top and fills in lines $3,7,11,15...$, then lines $2,6,10,14...$ and finally $4,8,12,16...$. At each stage of the uncompleted image, the software can interpolate missing information only crudely—so the first pass looks like a wall of colored blocks, and then the blocks get smaller and smaller until they are only one pixel wide, and the image is done.

Figure 8-8: *From top to bottom, this page by The Exploratorium shows how a four-pass interlaced GIF develops.*

A shareware application called WINGIF does the interlacing for you and a lot more besides. Simply open your GIF file into WINGIF, then choose File/Save and click the Format>> button in the dialog box. Pop the radio button to save in GIF format and also check the check box just to the left for Interlace GIF. Very simple. WINGIF is available on the online companion to this book, and at the following address:

ftp.best.com/pub/craig/windows_apps

The file is wingif14.zip, and it's shareware, so if you like it, you owe Kyle Powell $15.

Transparent Colors

An inline GIF has to have a rectangular shape—there's no way around that—but that doesn't mean it has to *look* rectangular. You can use an internal border of any irregular shape you like, and so long as everything outside that border is one unique color, you can declare that color to be transparent. A transparent color takes on the hue of whatever surrounds it on the browser screen. This treatment is much used for those little decorative balls that Web authors like to use for list bullets instead of boring old black blobs, but Figure 8-9 shows a much more imaginative use. LView Pro is one application that will do this trick for you, but Word IA's Web browser does not yet display transparent GIFs. Learn more about see-through colors at this address:

http://dragon.jpl.nasa.gov/~adam/transparent.html

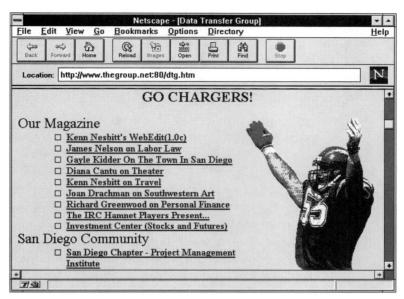

Figure 8-9: *This special page designed by Mark Burgess for the 1995 Superbowl shows creative use of a transparent .gif. It didn't seem to help, however.*

Drive-in Imaging Services

A company called Visioneering Research Laboratory, Inc., of Las Cruces, New Mexico, runs an intriguing online service called the Imaging Machine. Enter the URL of a GIF that's already on the Web, and the Imaging Machine offers you a whole smörgasbord of image-manipulation services, including interlacing by the ImageMagick application and transparency by GIFTRANS, then serves it up to order. If you like it, you can save it to disk, and you won't ever see an invoice from those nice people at VRL. Since this corporation is in business to make money, this "loss leader" will not last forever, we assume! Here's the address:

http://www.vrl.com:80/Imaging

Getting Ready to Post

Well, you've got your pages all dolled up now. Got your interlaced GIFs, your sensitive maps, your peacock-feather background and your blinking text. Now it's time to go public. Before you take the final step, though, you need to get organized.

If you're going to copy your files individually, rather than as a whole directory structure, make a list of all the files you need for posting—including all your GIFs and icons and buttons. It's easy to miss one or two if you don't have a checklist. If you intend to post all the files in your main directory and subdirectories, you probably won't have to worry about this. But if you've got a lot of extraneous stuff in those directories, you might do a cleanup by copying the unnecessary files to another directory and then deleting them. Once you've done all this, it's time to do a thorough check of all your pages to make sure you didn't accidentally remove something you need.

Remember that the physical appearance of your pages is actually browser-dependent. So if you expect people to access the page with different Web browsers (and if you're on the Web, they will), try it out with as many different browsers as you can, as well as a few different computer platforms.

When it comes to actually posting your pages on the Web, the most important thing is to be sure that everything will work the way you planned. Before you go trotting off and hand files over to your Web access provider or system administrator, sit down and check everything over one more time thoroughly—and then check it once again. Follow all your links and make sure they go where they're supposed to.

So far the work you've done on your files has probably been in your own computer. All of your documents have a defined relationship to one another that you've established with relative links, and you must be careful to preserve these links when you transfer the files to the Web server. When you post your site on the World Wide Web, bear in mind that someone may be accessing your page from far around the planet. When John Q. Websurfer from South Africa visits the World Wide Widget Corporation via modem and decides to peruse the Widget Museum, he doesn't want to get stuck in those hostile Web territories known as Unable to Locate and Access Forbidden. It could put him right off our widgets forever.

If you set up your directory structure as we suggested in Chapter 2 (and as shown in Figure 2-3), your links will all bear a relationship to the default page in your main Web directory. The only page likely to be accessed with a complete URL by the visitor will be your home page. Every other link at your site is relative. A link to another page from your home page will be in the form */pages/next.htm*, which tells the server computer to go one level down to the *pages* subdirectory and find the document *next.htm*. The document *next* may use a graphic in the *images* subdirectory. That link will be in the form *../images/wow.gif*, which tells the computer to go up one level then down to the subdirectory *images* to find the file *wow.gif*. If your Web site does not retain the same structure, the server computer will not be able to find the file and will throw up those hostile messages you want to avoid.

Once you're all ready, copy your Web site to a disk or main server computer with the XCOPY command:

> XCOPY *.* /S [destination]

The [destination] is the directory on the Web server analogous to the main directory of your Web files on your computer, and the XCOPY command will copy the main directory (*.*) and all its subdirectories.

From here on out you're in the hands of your system administrator, whose job it is to see that the site's up and running and part of that great computer in the sky we call the Internet.

Moving On

We've come a long way now—all the way from designing our first home page to creating forms and interlacing GIFs. Maybe you haven't yet ventured as far as trying all these things, but you're beginning to imagine the possibilities as you develop your own Web site and design new projects that can take advantage of all the Web resources.

All that jargon that sounded so confusing at first has now just become part of your daily computer vocabulary. As you note Web sites you like and try out new things on your pages, your expertise will continue to grow. Look back at that graphic that charts the growth of the Web, at the start of Chapter 1. See that big curve heading upward? You're riding the wave now. See you on the Web!

About the Online Companion

The book you hold in your hands is really only the core of *HTML Publishing With Internet Assistant*. The full package from Ventana Press includes all the carefully organized data and software available to you on Ventana Online's Web server, through the *Internet Assistant Online Companion*.

Ventana Online offers information, software and access to Internet resources for computer users and Ventana customers. Among these offerings are the online companion archives for our press and media products. This valuable information is regularly updated, with new publications and Internet software added as they become available. (So check with us often!)

Perhaps one of the most valuable features of the *Internet Assistant Online Companion* is its software archive. Here, you'll find and be able to download the latest versions of the freely available software mentioned in the book. And with Ventana Online's helpful descriptions of the software, you'll know exactly what you're getting and why. So you won't download the software just to find you have no use for it.

The online companion also links you to the Ventana Library. There you'll find useful press and jacket information on a variety of Ventana Press offerings and coming attractions, and you'll be able to order online the books you want.

The *Internet Assistant Online Companion* represents Ventana Online's ongoing commitment to offer the most dynamic and exciting products possible. And soon Ventana Online will be adding more services, including more multimedia supplements, searchable indexes and sections of the book, reproduced and hyperlinked to the Internet resources they reference.

To access, connect via the World Wide Web to **http://www.vmedia.com/hpia.html**

APPENDIX

HTML Tags

This is a list of all the HTML 2.0 tags that are supported by Word IA. The tags that are indented in the list (for example, <BASE> is indented under <HEAD>. . .<HEAD>) may be used only within the sections under which they are indented.

Tag	Description
DOCUMENT LEVEL	
<HTML>. . .</HTML>	Defines an HTML document
<HEAD>. . .</HEAD>	Document header
<BASE>	Base URL
<ISINDEX>	Searchable document
<LINK>	Related documents
<META>	Hidden document information
<NEXTID>	Edit indexing
<TITLE>. . .</TITLE>	Document title
<BODY>. . .</BODY>	Document body
SECTION LEVEL	
<ADDRESS>. . .</ADDRESS>	Address info section
<PRE>. . .</PRE>	Preformatted section
<FORM>. . .</FORM>	Interactive form section
<INPUT>	Form field
<OPTION>. . .</OPTION>	Item in a SELECT list
<SELECT>. . .</SELECT>	List of options for a form field
<TEXTAREA>. . .</TEXTAREA>	Large form field

Tag	Description
PARAGRAPH LEVEL	
<BLOCKQUOTE>...</BLOCKQUOTE>	Citation (usually indented)
<HR>	Horizontal rule
<P>...</P>	Paragraph
<DL>...</DL>	Definition list
<DT>...</DT>	Definition list term
<DD>...</DD>	Definition list definition
<DIR>...</DIR>	Directory list
<LI>...</LI>	List item
<MENU>...</MENU>	Menu listing
<OL>...</OL>	Ordered (numbered) list
<UL>...</UL>	Unordered (bulleted) list
LINE LEVEL	
<A>...</A>	Hypertext anchor
 	Line break
<Hn>...</Hn>	Heading level n (n=1 thru 6)
<IMG>	Inline image
WORD LEVEL: LOGICAL (OR SEMANTIC) WORD FORMATTING	
<CITE>...</CITE>	Citation (usually italic)
<CODE>...</CODE>	Computer code (usually monospaced)
<EM>...</EM>	Emphasis (usually italic)
<KBD>...</KBD>	Keyboard input
<SAMP>...</SAMP>	Literal text
<STRONG>...</STRONG>	Emphasis (usually boldface)
<VAR>...</VAR>	Variable name (usually italic)
WORD LEVEL: PHYSICAL WORD FORMATTING	
<B>...</B>	Boldface
<I>...</I>	Italic
<TT>...</TT>	Teletype (monospaced typewriter font)

APPENDIX C

Special Symbols in HTML

HTML allows an extended set of symbols, which is based on the International Standards Organization's *Latin-1* set—basically the lower half of the table you see when you use Word 6.0's menu option Insert/Symbol.

Word IA expects you to use that symbol insert table for any of the special characters you may want to use in Web publishing, and the software takes care of translating them to the HTML equivalents listed here. You would need these coded versions if you were writing special characters into your source code, however.

Two different formats are recognized. All accented letters plus a few special symbols may be represented as *entities*. These are fairly easy to remember; for example, é for é is intuitive once you get the feel for it. A larger set of symbols is represented by numeric *character references*, which are far from intuitive and are not much used if an entity is also available for the symbol needed.

Char.	Entity	Numeric	Description
†		†	Dagger
‡		‡	Double dagger
ˆ		ˆ	Circumflex accent
‰		‰	Salinity sign
Š		Š	Uppercase S, haček
Œ		Œ	Uppercase OE diphthong
™		™	Trademark symbol
š		š	Lowercase s, haček

Char.	Entity	Numeric	Description
œ		&#156;	Lowercase oe diphthong
Ÿ		&#159;	Uppercase Y, umlaut
¡		&#161;	Inverted exclamation mark
¢		&#162;	Cent sign
£		&#163;	Pound sterling
¤		&#164;	General currency sign
¥		&#165;	Japanese yen
¦		&#166;	Broken vertical bar
§		&#167;	Section sign
¨		&#168;	Umlaut (diaeresis)
©	&copy;	&#169;	Copyright symbol
ª		&#170;	Feminine ordinal
«		&#171;	Left angle quote, guillemet left
¬		&#172;	Not sign
		&#173;	Soft hyphen
®	&reg;	&#174;	Registered trademark
¯		&#175;	Macron accent
°		&#176;	Degree
±		&#177;	Plus or minus
²		&#178;	Superscript two
³		&#179;	Superscript three
´		&#180;	Acute accent
µ		&#181;	Micro sign (Greek mu)
¶		&#182;	Paragraph sign
·		&#183;	Middle dot
¸		&#184;	Cedilla
¹		&#185;	Superscript one
º		&#186;	Masculine ordinal
»		&#187;	Right angle quote, guillemet right
¼		&#188;	Fraction one-fourth
½		&#189;	Fraction one-half
¾		&#190;	Fraction three-fourths
¿		&#191;	Inverted question mark
À	&Agrave;	&#192;	Uppercase A, grave accent
Á	&Aacute;	&#193;	Uppercase A, acute accent
Â	&Acirc;	&#194;	Uppercase A, circumflex accent
Ã	&Atilde;	&#195;	Uppercase A, tilde
Ä	&Auml;	&#196;	Uppercase A, umlaut
Å	&Aring;	&#197;	Uppercase A, ring
Æ	&Aelig;	&#198;	Uppercase AE, diphthong (ligature)

Char.	Entity	Numeric	Description
Ç	&Ccedil;	&#199;	Uppercase C, cedilla
È	&Egrave;	&#200;	Uppercase E, grave accent
É	&Eacute;	&#201;	Uppercase E, acute accent
Ê	&Ecirc;	&#202;	Uppercase E, circumflex accent
Ë	&Euml;	&#203;	Uppercase E, umlaut
Ì	&Igrave;	&#204;	Uppercase I, grave accent
Í	&Iacute;	&#205;	Uppercase I, acute accent
Î	&Icirc;	&#206;	Uppercase I, circumflex accent
Ï	&Iuml;	&#207;	Uppercase I, umlaut
Ð	&ETH;	&#208;	Uppercase ETH, Icelandic
Ñ	&Ntilde;	&#209;	Uppercase N, tilde
Ò	&Ograve;	&#210;	Uppercase O, grave accent
Ó	&Oacute;	&#211;	Uppercase O, acute accent
Ô	&Ocirc;	&#212;	Uppercase O, circumflex accent
Õ	&Otilde;	&#213;	Uppercase O, tilde
Ö	&Ouml;	&#214;	Uppercase O, umlaut
×		&#215;	Multiply sign
Ø	&Oslash;	&#216;	Uppercase O, slash
Ù	&Ugrave;	&#217;	Uppercase U, grave accent
Ú	&Uacute;	&#218;	Uppercase U, acute accent
Û	&Ucirc;	&#219;	Uppercase U, circumflex accent
Ü	&Uuml;	&#220;	Uppercase U, umlaut
Ý	&Yacute;	&#221;	Uppercase Y, acute accent
Þ	&THORN;	&#222;	Uppercase THORN, Icelandic
ß	&szlig;	&#223;	Lowercase sharp s, German (sz ligature)
à	&agrave;	&#225;	Lowercase a, grave accent
á	&aacute;	&#225;	Lowercase a, acute accent
â	&acirc;	&#226;	Lowercase a, circumflex accent
ã	&atilde;	&#227;	Lowercase a, tilde
ä	&auml;	&#228;	Lowercase a, umlaut
å	&aring;	&#229;	Lowercase a, ring
æ	&aelig;	&#230;	Lowercase ae diphthong (ligature)
ç	&ccedil;	&#231;	Lowercase c, cedilla
è	&egrave;	&#232;	Lowercase e, grave accent
é	&eacute;	&#233;	Lowercase e, acute accent
ê	&ecirc;	&#234;	Lowercase e, circumflex accent
ë	&euml;	&#235;	Lowercase e, umlaut
ì	&igrave;	&#236;	Lowercase i, grave accent
í	&iacute;	&#237;	Lowercase i, acute accent

Char.	Entity	Numeric	Description
î	&icirc;	&#238;	Lowercase i, circumflex accent
ï	&iuml;	&#239;	Lowercase i, umlaut
ð	&eth;	&#240;	Lowercase eth, Icelandic
ñ	&ntilde;	&#241;	Lowercase n, tilde
ò	&ograve;	&#242;	Lowercase o, grave accent
ó	&oacute;	&#243;	Lowercase o, acute accent
ô	&ocirc;	&#244;	Lowercase o, circumflex accent
õ	&otilde;	&#245;	Lowercase o, tilde
ö	&ouml;	&#246;	Lowercase o, umlaut
÷		&#247;	Division sign
ø	&oslash;	&#248;	Lowercase o, slash
ù	&ugrave;	&#249;	Lowercase u, grave accent
ú	&uacute;	&#250;	Lowercase u, acute accent
û	&ucirc;	&#251;	Lowercase u, circumflex accent
ü	&uuml;	&#252;	Lowercase u, umlaut
ý	&yacute;	&#253;	Lowercase y, acute accent
þ	&thorn;	&#254;	Lowercase thorn, Icelandic
ÿ	&yuml;	&#255;	Lowercase y, umlaut
			Nonbreaking space

Note 1: Conventions for complete sets of mathematical and Greek symbols are in preparation for HTML 3.0.

Note 2: The literal strings © and ® are conventions of Netscape Communications Corporation, and are not recognized by Word IA or most other browsers.

In addition to the extended characters, four keyboard characters have special meanings in HTML and therefore need to be encoded as entities if the intention is to display them literally. Again, Word IA's software takes care of this translation for you unless you are working at source code level. They are as follows:

Char.	Entity	Numeric	Description
<	&lt;	&#60;	Less than sign
>	&gt;	&#62;	Greater than sign
&	&amp;	&#38;	Ampersand
"	&quot;	&#34;	Double quote sign

Designer Colors for the Web

O n the Web, colors are specified by their red/green/blue components. Each component color may be present in any intensity from 0 to 255. Hexadecimal numbers (see "Glossary") are convenient for specifying color components, because the 0–255 range in decimal becomes 00–ff in hexadecimal, requiring only two digits. Thus, in this convention, #000000 is pure black and #ffffff is pure white.

This partial list suggests which colors are created by some #rrggbb strings in between those two extremes. These strings may be used to specify Web page colors—for example, in the HTML code <BODY BGCOLOR="#5f929e"> to make a cadet blue background.

Color	#rrggbb
alice blue	#f0f8ff
antique white	#faebd7
antique white1	#ffefdb
antique white2	#eedfcc
antique white3	#cdc0b0
antique white4	#8b8378
aquamarine	#32bfc1
aquamarine1	#7fffd4
aquamarine2	#76eec6
aquamarine3	#66cdaa
aquamarine4	#458b74
azure1	#f0ffff
azure2	#e0eeee
azure3	#c1cdcd

azure4	#838b8b
beige	#f5f5dc
bisque1	#ffe4c4
bisque2	#eed5b7
bisque3	#cdb79e
bisque4	#8b7d6b
blanched almond	#ffebcd
blue1	#0000ff
blue2	#0000ee
blue3	#0000cd
blue4	#00008b
blue-violet	#8a2be2
brown	#a52a2a
brown1	#ff4040
brown2	#ee3b3b

Color	#rrggbb
brown3	#cd3333
brown4	#8b2323
burlywood	#deb887
burlywood1	#ffd39b
burlywood2	#eec591
burlywood3	#cdaa7d
burlywood4	#8b7355
cadet blue	#5f929e
cadet blue1	#98f5ff
cadet blue2	#8ee5ee
cadet blue3	#7ac5cd
cadet blue4	#53868b
chartreuse1	#7fff00
chartreuse2	#76ee00
chartreuse3	#66cd00
chartreuse4	#458b00
chocolate	#d2691e
chocolate1	#ff7f24
chocolate2	#ee7621
chocolate3	#cd661d
chocolate4	#8b4513
coral1	#ff7256
coral2	#ee6a50
coral3	#cd5b45
coral4	#8b3e2f
cornflower blue	#222298
cornsilk1	#fff8dc
cornsilk2	#eee8cd
cornsilk3	#cdc8b1
cornsilk4	#8b8878
cyan1	#00ffff
cyan2	#00eeee
cyan3	#00cdcd
cyan4	#008b8b
dark	#bdb76b
dark goldenrod	#b8860b
dark goldenrod1	#ffb90f
dark goldenrod2	#eead0e
dark goldenrod3	#cd950c
dark goldenrod4	#8b6508
dark green	#00562d
dark khaki	#bdb76b
dark nessy	#de00a5
dark olivegreen	#55562f
dark olivegreen1	#caff70
dark olivegreen2	#bcee68
dark olivegreen3	#a2cd5a
dark olivegreen4	#6e8b3d
dark orange	#ff8c00
dark orange1	#ff7f00
dark orange2	#ee7600
dark orange3	#cd6600
dark orange4	#8b4500
dark orchid	#8b208b
dark orchid1	#bf3eff
dark orchid2	#b23aee
dark orchid3	#9a32cd
dark orchid4	#68228b
dark salmon	#e9967a
dark seagreen	#8fbc8f
dark seagreen1	#c1ffc1
dark seagreen2	#b4eeb4
dark seagreen3	#9bcd9b
dark seagreen4	#698b69
dark slate blue	#384b66
dark slate gray	#2f4f4f
dark slate gray1	#97ffff
dark slate gray2	#8deeee
dark slate gray3	#79cdcd
dark slate gray4	#528b8b
dark turquoise	#00a6a6
dark violet	#9400d3
deep pink1	#ff1493
deep pink2	#ee1289
deep pink3	#cd1076
deep pink4	#8b0a50
deep skyblue1	#00bfff
deep skyblue2	#00b2ee
deep skyblue3	#009acd
deep skyblue4	#00688b
dodger blue1	#1e90ff

Color	#rrggbb
dodger blue2	#1c86ee
dodger blue3	#1874cd
dodger blue4	#104e8b
firebrick	#8e2323
firebrick1	#ff3030
firebrick2	#ee2c2c
firebrick3	#cd2626
firebrick4	#8b1a1a
floral white	#fffaf0
forest green	#509f69
gainsboro	#dcdcdc
ghost white	#f8f8ff
gold	#daaa00
gold1	#ffd700
gold2	#eec900
gold3	#cdad00
gold4	#8b7500
goldenrod	#efdf84
goldenrod1	#ffc125
goldenrod2	#eeb422
goldenrod3	#cd9b1d
goldenrod4	#8b6914
gray	**
green1	#00ff00
green2	#00ee00
green3	#00cd00
green4	#008b00
green-yellow	#adff2f
honeydew1	#f0fff0
honeydew2	#e0eee0
honeydew3	#c1cdc1
honeydew4	#838b83
hot pink	#ff69b4
hot pink1	#ff6eb4
hot pink2	#ee6aa7
hot pink3	#cd6090
hot pink4	#8b3a62

indian red	#6b3939
indian red1	#ff6a6a
indian red2	#ee6363
indian red3	#cd5555
indian red4	#8b3a3a
ivory1	#fffff0
ivory2	#eeeee0
ivory3	#cdcdc1
ivory4	#8b8b83
khaki	#b3b37e
khaki1	#fff68f
khaki2	#eee685
khaki3	#cdc673
khaki4	#8b864e
lavender	#e6e6fa
lavender blush1	#fff0f5
lavender blush2	#eee0e5
lavender blush3	#cdc1c5
lavender blush4	#8b8386
lawn green	#7cfc00
lemon chiffon1	#fffacd
lemon chiffon2	#eee9bf
lemon chiffon3	#cdc9a5
lemon chiffon4	#8b8970
light	#f08080
light blue	#b0e2ff
light blue1	#bfefff
light blue2	#b2dfee
light blue3	#9ac0cd
light blue4	#68838b
light coral	#f08080
light cyan1	#e0ffff
light cyan2	#d1eeee
light cyan3	#b4cdcd
light cyan4	#7a8b8b
light goldenrod	#eedd82
light goldenrod1	#ffec8b
light goldenrod2	#eedc82

** Any string defining equal red/green/blue components produces a gray. Thus, there are 254 gray levels available, from #010101 (one shade lighter than black) to #fefefe (one shade darker than white).

Color	#rrggbb
light goldenrod3	#cdbe70
light goldenrod4	#8b814c
light goldenrod-yellow	#fafad2
light nessy	#ff80d2
light pink	#ffb6c1
light pink1	#ffaeb9
light pink2	#eea2ad
light pink3	#cd8c95
light pink4	#8b5f65
light salmon1	#ffa07a
light salmon2	#ee9572
light salmon3	#cd8162
light salmon4	#8b5742
light seagreen	#20b2aa
light sky blue	#87cefa
light sky blue1	#b0e2ff
light sky blue2	#a4d3ee
light sky blue3	#8db6cd
light sky blue4	#607b8b
light slate blue	#8470ff
light slate gray	#778899
light steel blue	#7c98d3
light steel blue1	#cae1ff
light steel blue2	#bcd2ee
light steel blue3	#a2b5cd
light steel blue4	#6e7b8b
light yellow1	#ffffe0
light yellow2	#eeeed1
light yellow3	#cdcdb4
light yellow4	#8b8b7a
lime green	#00af14
linen	#faf0e6
magenta1	#ff00ff
magenta2	#ee00ee
magenta3	#cd00cd
magenta4	#8b008b
maroon	#8f0052
maroon1	#ff34b3
maroon2	#ee30a7

Color	#rrggbb
maroon3	#cd2990
maroon4	#8b1c62
medium	#d1c166
medium aquamarine	#00938f
medium blue	#3232cc
medium forest green	#32814b
medium goldenrod	#d1c166
medium orchid	#bd52bd
medium orchid1	#e066ff
medium orchid2	#d15fee
medium orchid3	#b452cd
medium orchid4	#7a378b
medium purple	#9370db
medium purple1	#ab82ff
medium purple2	#9f79ee
medium purple3	#8968cd
medium purple4	#5d478b
medium sea green	#347766
medium slate blue	#6a6a8d
medium spring green	#238e23
medium turquoise	#00d2d2
medium violet-red	#d52079
midnight blue	#2f2f64
mint cream	#f5fffa
misty rose1	#ffe4e1
misty rose2	#eed5d2
misty rose3	#cdb7b5
misty rose4	#8b7d7b
moccasin	#ffe4b5
navajo white1	#ffdead
navajo white2	#eecfa1
navajo white3	#cdb38b
navajo white4	#8b795e
navy blue	#232375
nessy	#ff42d2
old lace	#fdf5e6
olive drab	#6b8e23
olive drab1	#c0ff3e

Color	#rrggbb
olive drab2	#b3ee3a
olive drab3	#9acd32
olive drab4	#698b22
orange1	#ffa500
orange2	#ee9a00
orange3	#cd8500
orange4	#8b5a00
orange-red1	#ff4500
orange-red2	#ee4000
orange-red3	#cd3700
orange-red4	#8b2500
orchid	#ef84ef
orchid1	#ff83fa
orchid2	#ee7ae9
orchid3	#cd69c9
orchid4	#8b4789
pale	#73de78
pale goldenrod	#eee8aa
pale green	#73de78
pale green1	#9aff9a
pale green2	#90ee90
pale green3	#7ccd7c
pale green4	#548b54
pale turquoise	#afeeee
pale turquoise1	#bbffff
pale turquoise2	#aeeeee
pale turquoise3	#96cdcd
pale turquoise4	#668b8b
pale violet-red	#db7093
pale violet-red1	#ff82ab
pale violet-red2	#ee799f
pale violet-red3	#cd6889
pale violet-red4	#8b475d
papaya	#ffefd5
peach puff1	#ffdab9
peach puff2	#eecbad
peach puff3	#cdaf95
peach puff4	#8b7765
peru	#cd853f
pink1	#ffb5c5

Color	#rrggbb
pink2	#eea9b8
pink3	#cd919e
pink4	#8b636c
plum	#c5489b
plum1	#ffbbff
plum2	#eeaeee
plum3	#cd96cd
plum4	#8b668b
powder blue	#b0e0e6
purple	#a020f0
purple1	#9b30ff
purple2	#912cee
purple3	#7d26cd
purple4	#551a8b
red1	#ff0000
red2	#ee0000
red3	#cd0000
red4	#8b0000
rosy brown	#bc8f8f
rosy brown1	#ffc1c1
rosy brown2	#eeb4b4
rosy brown3	#cd9b9b
rosy brown4	#8b6969
royal blue	#4169e1
royal blue1	#4876ff
royal blue2	#436eee
royal blue3	#3a5fcd
royal blue4	#27408b
saddle brown	#8b4513
salmon	#e9967a
salmon1	#ff8c69
salmon2	#ee8262
salmon3	#cd7054
salmon4	#8b4c39
sandy brown	#f4a460
sea green	#529584
sea green1	#54ff9f
sea green2	#4eee94
sea green3	#43cd80
sea green4	#2e8b57
seashell1	#fff5ee

Color	#rrggbb
seashell2	#eee5de
seashell3	#cdc5bf
seashell4	#8b8682
sienna	#96522d
sienna1	#ff8247
sienna2	#ee7942
sienna3	#cd6839
sienna4	#8b4726
sky blue	#729fff
sky blue1	#87ceff
sky blue2	#7ec0ee
sky blue3	#4a708b
slate blue	#7e88ab
slate blue1	#836fff
slate blue2	#7a67ee
slate blue3	#6959cd
slate blue4	#473c8b
slate gray	#708090
slate gray1	#c6e2ff
slate gray2	#b9d3ee
slate gray3	#9fb6cd
slate gray4	#6c7b8b
snow1	#fffafa
snow2	#eee9e9
snow3	#cdc9c9
snow4	#8b8989
spring green	#41ac41
spring green1	#00ff7f
spring green2	#00ee76
spring green3	#00cd66
spring green4	#008b45
steel blue	#5470aa
steel blue1	#63b8ff
steel blue2	#5cacee
steel blue3	#4f94cd
steel blue4	#36648b

Color	#rrggbb
tan	#deb887
tan1	#ffa54f
tan2	#ee9a49
tan3	#cd853f
tan4	#8b5a2b
thistle	#d8bfd8
thistle1	#ffe1ff
thistle2	#eed2ee
thistle3	#cdb5cd
thistle4	#8b7b8b
tomato1	#ff6347
tomato2	#ee5c42
tomato3	#cd4f39
tomato4	#8b3626
transparent	#000001
turquoise	#19ccdf
turquoise1	#00f5ff
turquoise2	#00e5ee
turquoise3	#00c5cd
turquoise4	#00868b
violet	#9c3ece
violet-red	#f33e96
violet-red1	#ff3e96
violet-red2	#ee3a8c
violet-red3	#cd3278
violetred4	#8b2252
wheat	#f5deb3
wheat1	#ffe7ba
wheat2	#eed8ae
wheat3	#cdba96
wheat4	#8b7e66
white smoke	#f5f5f5
yellow1	#ffff00
yellow2	#eeee00
yellow3	#cdcd00
yellow4	#8b8b00
yellow-green	#32d838

Glossary

Anchor   In hypertext, the object that is highlighted and "clickable." It may be a word, a phrase or an inline image. When selected by a user, the destination object is loaded.

Anonymous FTP   An FTP service that serves any user, not just users having accounts at the site. Anonymous FTP generally permits downloading of all files, but uploading only into a directory called /incoming.

Archie   A keyword-search service that searches the directory and file titles of all FTP sites that are indexed.

ASCII (American Standard Code for Information Interchange)   A standard coding of letters, numbers and symbols. An ASCII file is one that makes use of only the first 128 ASCII symbols—the symbols you see on your keyboard, basically. The advantage of ASCII files is that one bit per byte is always available for purposes such as error checking.

.au   In hypermedia, an audio file format common in DOS systems.

Backbone   The connections between the primary computers in a network. Stub networks branch off the backbone.

Bandwidth   Used (somewhat inaccurately) to express the maximum possible throughput of a data link in bits per second. A so-called T1 line has a bandwidth of 1.544 megabits per second (mbps).

Binary   In computing, a numbering system that has two as its base. Unlike an ASCII file, a binary file makes use of 256 symbols and so does not keep a bit free for error checking.

Bookmark   Hidden identity tag placed in a Word or HTML document, enabling that point in the document to be a hyperlink destination.

Cache   (1) An area of random access memory (RAM) set aside to hold data or instructions that would normally be read from disk, in order to speed up access to it. (2) In network operation, an area of the disk set aside to hold data that would normally be read from the net, for the same reason.

Callout   In graphics, an explanatory label added to a picture or figure. As an example, Figure 7-3 of this book has six callouts explaining the button functions on the Forms toolbar.

Callout leader   The line leading from a callout to the part of the picture it relates to.

Chameleon   A commercial Internet package designed specifically for the Windows environment by NetManage of Cupertino, CA.

Client/server software   An arrangement of computers, very common in Internet systems, whereby a small system called the client makes use of the data management services of a much larger computer, the server. Word IA's Web browser is a client/server system, with the client running on your machine taking advantage of the far greater processing power of the server at a remote site.

Cyberspace   Fanciful term coined by William Gibson in the novel *Neuromancer* to describe the sum total of computer-accessible information in the world.

Decimal tab   In graphic design, a type of tab setting that is used to correctly align columns of numbers.

Destination   In hypertext, the object (document, picture or media file) that is loaded when the user selects an anchor.

Dial-up account   The type of Internet access account that is connected only when a modem connection is established, as distinct from a direct permanent connection. This is used to specify a shell account as opposed to SLIP- or PPP-type access, even though SLIP or PPP accounts are frequently also established by dial-up.

Direct connection   A hardwired connection between a computer and the Internet, giving the computer an IP address and the ability to function as a Web site.

DNS (Domain Name Server)   Software that converts host names to IP addresses.

Drop cap   In graphic design, a large decorative letter at the start of a paragraph that occupies the height of several lines of text.

Entity   In HTML, a string such as ç that is displayed as a non-keyboard symbol (in this case, ç).

Eudora   A popular e-mail manager developed by Qualcomm Inc. of San Diego.

.exe   In DOS, this file extension denotes an "executable" file that will run if its name is simply entered at the DOS prompt (with or without the .exe). Files that are executable in Windows also frequently have the extension .exe.

External image   An image that may be accessed by a hypertext link from an HTML page, but is not automatically displayed when the page loads, as is an inline image.

FAQ (Frequently Asked Questions)   Pronounced "fak," shorthand for an information file about some system.

Favorite list   A personal list of favorite Web addresses that creates hypertext links to the addresses. Other Web browsers call this a Hotlist (Mosaic) or a Bookmark list (Netscape).

Fire wall   Software application that isolates a local network from the Internet, effectively preventing unauthorized entry to the network. Legitimate communication through a fire wall has to be carried out via a proxy.

Flame   A deliberately abusive message in e-mail or a newsgroup posting. What may happen to those who fail to read the FAQ.

FTP (File Transfer Protocol)   One of the original protocols on the Internet, which allows for very efficient transfer of entire data files between computers but discourages interactive browsing.

GIF (Graphics Interchange Format)   One of many formats for computerized images, designed to be highly transportable between computer systems. Sometimes referred to as "Compuserve" after the company that first devised it. Almost invariably used for inline images in Web pages.

Gopher   An Internet search and display application that reduces all Internet resource "trees" to onscreen menus.

Greek   In desktop publishing, an approximate representation of text used when there is insufficient screen space to show it in properly readable form. By extension, any onscreen text that is garbled.

Hexadecimal numbering   A numbering system using 16 as the base instead of 10. The first 16 hexadecimal numbers are 1,2,3,4,5,6,7,8,9,A,B,C,D,E,F,10. This system is more useful than the decimal system in the world of digital computers because translation from a hexadecimal number to its binary (base 2) equivalent is very easy, whereas decimal-to-binary translations are clumsy and error-prone.

Home page   (1) The page a Web browser user has designated to load automatically at startup. (2) A personal page you control and refer other people to.

Host   A computer whose primary function is facilitating communications.

Hotlist   A personal list of favorite Web addresses that creates hypertext links to the addresses. Same as a Favorite list.

HTML (HyperText Markup Language)   A convention for inserting tags into a text file that Web browsers like Netscape can interpret to display or link to hypermedia. HTML files are all ASCII, and usually have the extension .html or .htm.

Hypermedia   Media such as video and audio, which go beyond what was thought (not so very long ago!) to be the realm of personal computer display.

Hypertext   System of interactive text linking that allows the reader to choose any path through the sum total of available text.

HyperText Transfer Protocol (HTTP)   Internationally agreed-upon system of computer data exchange for WWW files.

Inline image   On a Web page, an image to be loaded along with the page text (although inlines can be suppressed by a user to speed up page loading).

Internet   Network of computer networks stretching across the world, linking computers of many different types. No one organization has control of the Internet or jurisdiction over it.

InternetWorks   Graphical Web browser developed by BookLink Technologies, Inc., now owned by America Online (AOL) and made available to AOL clients. Also, the software that was teamed up with Word 6.0 to create Internet Assistant.

IP address   An Internet machine address formatted with numbers rather than a host name. An IP (Internet Protocol) address may also contain a port number, separated from the host address by a colon.

JPEG (Joint Photographic Experts Group)   An image file format allowing for a choice of three levels of file compression, with progressive tradeoff of image quality.

Link   In World Wide Web context, short for "hypertext link," meaning a path a user may follow that connects one part of a document to another part of the same document, a different document or some other resource.

Local area network (LAN)   Hardwired network of computer terminals that share resources but are restricted to one site or close group of sites.

Lynx   Name of a text-only World Wide Web browser, available for UNIX, Linux, DOS and a few other operating systems.

MIME (Multipurpose Internet Mail Extensions)   A set of agreed-upon formats enabling binary files to be sent as e-mail or attached to e-mail. *MIME types* has come to mean hypermedia formats in general, even when not communicated by e-mail.

Mirror site   A subsidiary FTP site that has the same content as the main site that it reflects. Used to take the load off sites that are so popular they are frequently inaccessible because of congestion.

Mosaic   The first World Wide Web graphical browser. (See also NCSA.)

MPEG (Motion Picture Experts Group)   Modern standard format for compression and storage of video hypermedia files.

NCSA (National Center for Supercomputing Applications)   A US government center at the University of Illinois. NCSA developed the Mosaic Web browser and other Internet interfaces and offers many services to HTML authors.

Newt   The TCP/IP part of Chameleon. Newt can be used to establish a SLIP or PPP Internet connection for Netscape.

Packet switching   A system used extensively throughout the Internet for handling messages. Based on the breakdown of a message into standardized packets, each of which is independently routed to the addressee.

Pixel   Smallest possible dot of solid color in an electronic picture.

PPP (Point-to-Point Protocol) A convention for transmitting packet-switched data.

Protocol In computer communications, an agreed-upon set of rules for data exchange.

Proxy A software service used to access the Internet around a fire wall put up to ensure security in a large system.

QuickTime A hypermedia video format, invented for Macintosh multimedia systems but now also available for DOS/Windows.

Search engine A keyword-searching algorithm or a complete software package that includes search algorithms.

Server The server half of a client/server pair: the computer that handles the primary data management tasks on behalf of its clients.

Shell A simple, usually menu-driven interface that shields a computer user from the complexities of operating systems such as UNIX. Hence a common type of Internet connection, known as a UNIX shell account, can be operated efficiently with extremely limited actual knowledge of UNIX.

SLIP (Serial Line Internet Protocol) A convention for transmitting packet-switched data.

Snail mail Somewhat disparaging term used by devotees of the speed of e-mail. It simply means ordinary post office mail.

Socket One of a series of memory addresses in a computer reserved for data exchange with a TCP/IP stack.

Source document In the World Wide Web, the raw ASCII file that an HTML author creates, as distinct from a Web page, which is the representation of a source document in hypertext.

Stack In the context of TCP/IP, the ordered series of protocols and packet drivers required to interface a desktop computer with the Internet.

Tag   Name given to the code strings embedded in HTML documents, such as <H1>.

TCP/IP (Transmission Control Protocol/Internet Protocol)
Shorthand for the most common packet-switching protocols used on the Internet.

Telnet   A software system that establishes a connection between two computers for the purpose of data exchange. Unlike FTP, TELNET is interactive and, as commonly used, makes a desktop computer behave as though it were the workstation of a much larger computer.

TIFF (Tagged Image File Format)   A standard format for storing hypermedia image files. A .tiff file is generally uncompressed (and therefore large) and can contain many images.

Trumpet Winsock   A popular Winsock package (TCP/IP stack interface) designed by Peter Tattam of the University of Tasmania. (See also Winsock.)

UNIX   The operating system of choice for computers dedicated to the Internet. UNIX is inherently suited to network operations.

URL (Uniform Resource Locator)   An address that completely defines a resource of the World Wide Web. A URL has five elements:

- the service—http or ftp or a few others
- the host—the computer that handles the resource
- the port number (defaults according to the service requested)
- the path to the directory containing the resource
- the file name of the resource

The format of a URL is *service://host:port/path/filename*.

WAV   A standard format for storing hypermedia audio (.wav) files.

Web   Short for World Wide Web.

Web browser   User interface to the Web. InternetWorks, Mosaic and Netscape are examples of graphical Web browsers.

Web crawler   Software that searches the Web (or more commonly, a database derived from the Web) for keywords input by a user.

Webmaster   Person at a Web server site who is qualified to administer all Web resources at that site.

Web page   Coherent document that is readable by a Web browser. A Web page may vary in complexity all the way from a simple piece of text enclosed by the HTML tags <PRE>. . .</PRE>, meaning "preformatted," to a densely coded HTML file giving the user access to many types of hypermedia.

Web server   A server computer equipped to offer World Wide Web access to its clients.

Web spider   A type of keyword-search software.

Winsock   Short for Windows Sockets, the interface between your Web browser and the TCP/IP stack you are running.

Wizard   Boilerplate document available to Word 6.0 users as a menu option. An example would be a preformatted invoice that needs only simple customization to be ready to print as a sophisticated piece of desktop publishing.

World Wide Web   Arrangement of Internet-accessible resources, including hypertext and hypermedia, addressed by URLs.

Index

C

D

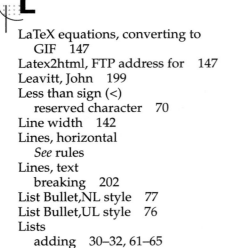

Z

Colophon

HTML Publishing With Internet Assistant was produced on a Power Mac 8100/80. Page proofs were printed on a Hewlett Packard LaserJet 4M Plus.

PageMaker 5.0 was used for all layout. The body copy is Adobe Palatino. Subheads are set in Bembo. Chapter titles and running heads are set in Adobe Univers. Tables are set in Adobe Franklin Gothic.

Internet Resources

The Windows Internet Tour Guide, Second Edition 🌐

$29.95, 424 pages, illustrated

This runaway bestseller has been updated to include
Ventana Mosaic™, the hot new Web reader, along with
graphical software for e-mail, file downloading,
newsreading and more. Noted for its down-to-earth
documentation, the new edition features expanded listings
and a look at new Net developments. Includes three
companion disks.

Internet E-Mail Quick Tour 🌐

$14.00, 152 pages, illustrated

Whether it's the Internet or an online service, most people
use their connections primarily for electronic messaging.
This all-in-one guide to getting it right includes tips on
software, security, style and Netiquette. Also included: how
to obtain an e-mail account, useful addresses, interesting
mailing lists and more!

Mosaic Quick Tour for Windows, Special Edition 🌐

$24.95, 224 pages, illustrated

A national bestseller straight out of the gate in its first edition,
thanks to its down-to-earth approach to Mosaic™—the "killer
app" that changed the face of the Internet. The Web, with its
audio, video and graphic capabilities and hyperlinks between
sites, comes to life in this important update that focuses on
Ventana Mosaic™, the newly standardized commercial
version of the most famous free software in the world. Includes
information on audio and video components of Ventana
Mosaic, along with a guide to top Web attractions. Two
companion disks feature Ventana Mosaic and Win32s
required to run the program.

Internet Virtual Worlds Quick Tour
$14.00, 224 pages, illustrated

Learn to locate and master real-time interactive communication forums and games by participating in the virtual worlds of MUD (Multi-User Dimension) and MOO (MUD Object-Oriented). *Internet Virtual Worlds Quick Tour* introduces users to the basic functions by defining different categories (individual, interactive and both) and detailing standard protocols. Also revealed is the insider's lexicon of these mysterious cyberworlds.

Internet Roadside Attractions
$29.95, 376 pages, illustrated

Why take the word of one when you can get a quorum? Seven experienced Internauts—teachers and bestselling authors—share their favorite Web sites, Gophers, FTP sites, chats, games, newsgroups and mailing lists. Organized alphabetically by category for easy browsing with in-depth descriptions. The companion CD-ROM contains the entire text of the book, hyperlinked for off-line browsing and online Web hopping.

Internet Chat Quick Tour
$14.00, 200 pages, illustrated

Global conversations in real-time are an integral part of the Internet. The worldwide chat network is where users find online help and forums on the latest scientific research. The *Internet Chat Quick Tour* describes the best software sites for users to chat on a variety of subjects.

Books marked with this logo include a free Internet *Online Companion™*, featuring archives of free utilities plus a software archive and links to other Internet resources.

Looking Good With QuarkXPress

$34.95, 544 pages, illustrated

Looking Good With QuarkXPress showcases the graphic devices, layouts and design tools built into the latest version of QuarkXPress. The basic principles of graphic design are brought to life on every page with examples of newsletters, brochures and more in a straightforward guide that is accessible to users at all levels. The companion CD-ROM features valuable templates, fonts, clip art, backgrounds and XTensions for both Macintosh and Windows users.

Advertising From the Desktop

$24.95, 464 pages, illustrated

Advertising From the Desktop offers unmatched design advice and helpful how-to instructions for creating persuasive ads. With tips on how to choose fonts, select illustrations, apply special effects and more, this book is an idea-packed resource for improving the looks and effects of your ads.

Newsletters From the Desktop, Second Edition

$24.95, 392 pages, illustrated

Now the millions of desktop publishers who produce newsletters can learn how to improve the designs of their publications. Filled with helpful design tips and illustrations, as well as hands-on tips for building a great-looking publication. Includes an all-new color gallery of professionally designed newsletters, offering desktop publishers at all levels a wealth of ideas and inspiration.

To order any Ventana Press title, complete this order form and mail or fax it to us, with payment, for quick shipment.

TITLE	ISBN	Quantity		Price		Total
Advertising From the Desktop	1-56604-064-7	_____	x	$24.95	=	$ _____
Internet Chat Quick Tour	1-56604-223-2	_____	x	$14.00	=	$ _____
Internet E-Mail Quick Tour	1-56604-220-8	_____	x	$14.00	=	$ _____
Internet Roadside Attractions	1-56604-193-7	_____	x	$29.95	=	$ _____
Internet Virtual Worlds Quick Tour	1-56604-222-4	_____	x	$14.00	=	$ _____
Looking Good in Color	1-56604-219-4	_____	x	$29.95	=	$ _____
Looking Good in Print, 3rd Edition	1-56604-047-7	_____	x	$24.95	=	$ _____
Looking Good With QuarkXPress	1-56604-148-1	_____	x	$34.95	=	$ _____
Mosaic Quick Tour for Windows, Special Edition	1-56604-214-3	_____	x	$24.95	=	$ _____
Newsletters From the Desktop, 2nd Edition	1-56604-133-3	_____	x	$24.95	=	$ _____
Publishing on the Internet for Windows	1-56604-229-1	_____	x	$49.95	=	$ _____
The Presentation Design Book, 2nd Edition	1-56604-014-0	_____	x	$24.95	=	$ _____
Walking the World Wide Web	1-56604-208-9	_____	x	$29.95	=	$ _____
The Windows Internet Tour Guide, 2nd Edition	1-56604-174-0	_____	x	$29.95	=	$ _____
				Subtotal	=	$ _____
				Shipping	=	$ _____
				TOTAL	=	$ _____

SHIPPING:

For all standard orders, please ADD $4.50/first book, $1.35/each additional.
For Internet Membership Kit orders, ADD $6.50/first kit, $2.00/each additional.
For "two-day air," on books, ADD $8.25/first book, $2.25/each additional.
For "two-day air" on the IMK, ADD $10.50/first kit, $4.00/each additional.
For orders to Canada, ADD $6.50/book.
For orders sent C.O.D., ADD $4.50 to your shipping rate.
North Carolina residents must ADD 6% sales tax.
International orders require additional shipping charges.

Name _____ Daytime telephone _____

Company _____

Address (No PO Box) _____

City _____ State _____ Zip _____

____ Payment enclosed ____VISA ____MC Acc't # _____ Exp. date _____

Exact name on card _____ Signature _____

Mail to: Ventana Press, PO Box 2468, Chapel Hill, NC 27515 ☎ 919/942-0220 Fax 919/942-1140

Check your local bookstore or software retailer for these and other bestselling titles, or call toll free: **800/743-5369**